ARTIF INTELLIGENCE FOR BUSINESS:

HOW ARTIFICIAL INTELLIGENCE CAN BE APPLIED IN YOUR COMPANY, IN MARKETING AND HOW AI IS REVOLUTIONIZING OUR LIFE IN HEALTHCARE AND MEDICINE.

engaging in the rendering of legal, financial, medical or professional advice. The content within this book has been derived from various sources. Please consult a licensed professional before attempting any techniques outlined in this book.

By reading this document, the reader agrees that under no circumstances is the author responsible for any losses, direct or indirect, which are incurred as a result of the use of information contained within this document, including, but not limited to, — errors, omissions, or inaccuracies.

Table of Contents

Introduction

I'm excited that you have chosen to immerse yourself in the interesting world of Artificial Intelligence to help you in your business expansion. You will soon make discovery that there are various Artificial Intelligence applications that are in use in the modern world these apps are designed to help in making our everyday simpler and more productive.

Artificial Intelligence refers to the capability of digital computers or robots that are computer-controlled to carry out tasks normally linked with beings with high intelligent levels. AI is commonly used in the development of systems that are gifted with intellectual processes that characterize human beings i.e. the ability to discover meaning, learn, or generalize from experiences from the past. Demonstrations have shown that AI programmed computers or machines are well capable of handling very complex tasks.

Artificial Intelligence can be referred to as a concept in which a product, a robot, or a computer is made to think in a similar or a better manner than human beings. Artificial Intelligence (AI) in easy terms is the study of how the human brain thinks, learns, makes decisions and works, in the process of problem solving. The main goal of AI is in the improvement of computer functions directly related to the human knowledge i.e. problem-solving, learning and reasoning

The main goal of Artificial Intelligence even as it continues being incorporated in business is to have the ability to adapt to and learn from broader array of challenges. This will eventually eliminate the risk associated with limitation in regards to AI problem solving capabilities.

At the same time, it's important to remember that as much as there is the positive aspect regarding how Artificial Intelligence impacts business, AI also has some risks associated with it. These risks can be very detrimental in your business though many technocrats argue that the benefits outweigh the disadvantages.

Artificial Intelligence isn't targeted to act as a total replacement of human beings. AI only serves in augmenting our abilities as well as enabling us to perform our tasks in a better and more efficient manner. Machines that are fitted with AI applications learn in a different way as compared to human beings; this means that they analyse things in a different way. They are better placed to capture patterns and relationships that escape us.

Artificial intelligence does an incredible job in business as far as delivering accurate results is concerned. This is simply because machines aren't affected by external factors as they carry on their duties as is the normal occurrence in human beings.

The benefits that businesses are deriving from AI is immense. From machine learning software to deep learning tools, the opportunities the field of AI is presenting to the world of business is vast. Organizations are using AI to build a competitive edge within the marketplace. The importance is visible in highly competitive industries. For companies to benefit from AI, they have to invest in data mining software as data drives AI. Latter AI software combines data with algorithms to produce analytical models that businesses are using to make decisions.

In highly competitive industries, efficiency is improved using AI. The automation of processes allows for better customer experience for business clients. The automation may include AI software that can give insight on ways to improve operations. The knowledge from the comprehension assists companies to work on their operational weaknesses. Cloud computing, as an example, uses AI to negate the disadvantages of servers being present on business sites. There is AI software that helps businesses reduce their costs of operation. AI is helping organizations operationally by reducing human workload, therefore, allowing people to focus on core business operations.

The sales and marketing aspects of businesses are transforming by the advent of AI use. Individualized customer marketing is, now a reality. Targeted ads on websites and search engines are now part and parcel of today's marketing program for businesses. On the sales front, AI-backed CRM (Customer Relationship Management) software is commonplace as concerns working the sales process. These tools allow for aggregation of large amounts of data giving insights that were not previously available. Companies are using

AI-based beacons to personalize shopping experiences from pricing to offers. Marketing ads are now a staple on social media platforms.

The human resource aspect of businesses is benefitting from AI in a variety of ways. The development of AI is creating opportunities for businesses to access the global workforce at the touch of a button. Organizations are seeing a surge in the availability of freelance workers willing to work remotely for industries able to take advantage of the opportunity. The ability to work remotely can be a competitive edge for businesses and can be a way to reduce human resource costs, given the varied pay structures on a global scale.

Businesses are transforming how they interact with customers using AI-backed systems. Some companies have incorporated AI tools like chatbots as part of their customer care strategy. Studies are showing that the use of automated customer care tools is improving levels of customer engagement. Moreover, it can augment the human aspect of customer service with people taking over from the AI systems when the task is beyond the abilities of the AI software. AI systems are in use for follow up purposes on customers by businesses for cases that require feedback by the company to the client.

The most fascinating aspect is the use of AI systems in the medical sector; techniques from object recognition, image classification and deep learning are now being employed to spot cancer with similar accuracy as radiologists (through MRIs). Generally, there are several benefits that are directly linked to Artificial Intelligence as well a number of risks associated with the same. The main impact in the business world is the aspect of time saving and simplifying complex tasks.

There are several books on Artificial Intelligence as a Modern Approach to use in Businesses, thanks once again for picking this one! I have dedicated my time to ensure that it delivers as much information useful for your business as possible.

Chapter 1 The State of AI in Business

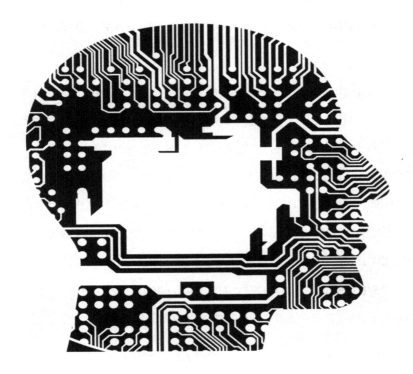

Prior to making any observations with regards to the manner in which technologies related to Artificial Intelligence are impacting the business fraternity, it's of great importance to have a good understanding of the Artificial Intelligence terms. AI is a general and broad term which denotes to any form of software in computers which performs humanlike activities. These activities may involve easy to complicated roles including planning to more complex ones like problem solving.

Artificial Intelligence is defined as the process in which machines replicate the processes of human intelligence. Some of the processes associated with human intelligence include self-correction, reasoning (making use of rules in reaching conclusions that are definite) and learning (process of acquiring information as well as rules that govern making use of these information). The AI has precise applications including; expert systems, speech recognition and machine vision.

AL is considered to be either strong Artificial Intelligence or weak Artificial Intelligence. Weak AI can also be referred to as the narrow AI; this is a system aimed and designed for precise tasks i.e. Apple's Siri. Strong AI is also known as general intelligence, a system that comprises of indiscriminate human intellectual abilities. When a task that isn't familiar is presented, the strong AI is tasked with finding a solution; this doesn't require intervention from human beings.

Since staffing, software and hardware costs for Artificial Intelligence can be very costly, many dealers are adding AI modules in their typical offerings. AI is also made accessible in the service platforms; this means that companies and individuals are permitted to try out with Artificial Intelligence for certain multiple platforms and purposes prior to making any commitments.

Some of the popular Artificial Intelligence cloud are as follows:

- Google AI
- IBM Watson Assistant
- Amazon AI

While the tools in Artificial Intelligence present a variety of functioning capabilities for many businesses, their use has raised ethical concerns. This is because these machines are programmed by human beings, which leads to the belief that there is bound to be a bias which needs close monitoring.

Some technocrats have come to the conclusion that Artificial Intelligence is a word that is linked closely to common culture; this has caused fears that are unrealistic in human beings concerning AI and the questionable expectations concerning how life and the workplace will experience change. Machines will only react and act like human beings only if they are well equipped with adequate information in relation to the present world.

Artificial Intelligence is a component in computer science in which the development machines that are gifted react and perform tasks like humans is emphasized. Some of the tasks intended to be performed by computers that have been installed with A.I are:

A. problem solving

B. Planning

C. Learning

D. Speech recognition

E. Ability to move and manipulate objects

F. Perception

Artificial Intelligence can be termed as a computer science branch whose aim is creating intelligent machines. This particular branch has become very vital in the technology industry.

The Subdisciplines of AI

AI is an umbrella term for cognitive technologies that mimic the intelligent behavior of humans, in some cases exceeding human limits. These technologies will become more pervasive in organizations, while humans work alongside them.

Fundamentally, think of everything that the human brain can do: its ability to recognize objects and faces, understand language, solve problems, control movement, experience emotions, etc. When AI researchers and technologists started to explore how the human brain works with the intent of creating a single system that functions like the brain, they soon realized the difficulty of such an exercise. No single system or set of algorithms was able to replicate the general functionality of the human brain.

Instead, researchers started looking at different subdisciplines to solve different problems. For example, humans can see with their eyes and recognize objects in their environment. This gave rise to the disciplines of image processing and computer vision. The goal of these disciplines was to build systems and software that could see as well as or better than humans can and could recognize objects in the scene by type.

In other words, researchers took the challenge of replicating the functions of the human brain and broke it down into narrowly focused disciplines to solve narrow problems. The ultimate idea was that once we developed and built all these individual systems, they could somehow be put together to achieve the same functions a human has. That is how we ended up with the many subdisciplines that come under the umbrella of AI.

The following is a list and brief explanation of some of these subdisciplines of AI:

- Pattern recognition is the science of being able to recognize patterns in data. This includes object recognition, pattern analysis in data, and handwritten character recognition.
- Machine learning is the science of being able to teach a computer to learn things so that it can respond to similar or new situations. This is unlike the programming paradigm where the programmer has to code all possible combinations of responses programmatically. Machine learning includes face recognition, playing games such as chess, and predicting the weather. Machine learning and pattern recognition share many algorithms.
- Cognitive computing is the science of problem solving, which considers many facts to come to conclusions. Cognitive computing includes logical derivations and processing lots of information to arrive at new conclusions, among other functions.
- Robotics is the science controlling mechanical objects in a nondeterministic environment through software. Robotics uses algorithms from other subdisciplines to react to the environment.

- Neural networks/deep learning is the science of replicating the neural structure of the human brain to achieve a wide range of abilities that humans are able to do. Recently this subdiscipline has been widely successful in replicating many functions of the human brain, such as being able to recognize objects and faces, learn new concepts, and even help make decisions.
- Natural language processing is the science of understanding and responding to human language. Applications include automated phone responses and voice-driven commands.
- Computer vision is the science of replicating human vision to recognize objects, see color, and identify visual patterns.
- Image processing is the science of processing digital images. This is often used as the first step in computer vision to process the individual pixels that make up an image. For example, to recognize an object, its outline has to first be figured out. After that, computer vision algorithms can try to decode what the outline represents.

Image processing algorithms also play a major role in face recognition.

- Associative memory is the science of replicating the human memory on one particular aspect of recall through association. This is useful for instantaneous recall when, say, we are picking out a known face from a crowd. Traditional computer memory uses sequential scans and address references.
- Genetic/evolutionary programming is the science of replicating human evolution on a fast timescale so that we can hope to get improvements over much iteration.

These subdisciplines make up the overarching discipline of AI. However, these are not siloed disciplines, as they borrow techniques and algorithms from one another to achieve different objectives. For example, to train a machine to recognize a known object such as an aircraft, we would likely use algorithms and techniques from image processing, computer vision, pattern recognition, and neural networks.

Recently, neural networks and a special adaptation of it called deep learning have gained much traction because of a push from companies like Google and Facebook. Successes in this subdiscipline have also encouraged more exploration.

In essence, AI is an umbrella of many disciplines and techniques that help to not only automate, but also provide predictive and cognitive abilities. With this technology, every aspect of business and every business will be impacted.

How is Artificial Intelligence Applied in Business?

Artificial intelligence has been known to be of great impact in the business sector for many years now; it's been in practice for decades. Nevertheless, due to the possibility of accessing huge amounts of data as well as increased processing speeds, Artificial Intelligence has also started taking root in our lives on a daily basis.

From image or voice recognition and language generation to driverless cars, machine learning and predictive analytics, AI systems are applied in various areas. The AI technologies are crucial in yielding innovation, reshaping the manner in which companies carry on with their operations and in the provision of new opportunities in business.

Artificial Intelligence is speedily becoming a tool that is being used competitively in business. It's very clear that companies are beyond negotiating about the advantages and disadvantages of Artificial Intelligence. From data analytics to customer service to arriving at predictive recommendations, AI is viewed by leaders in the business world as a very necessary tool.

Artificial Intelligence has been ranked among the top technologies that a company needs to utilize; this can be done by discovering how to make use of the AI technology to their advantage. There are several devices that we use in our everyday lives that are enabled by the Artificial Intelligence applications i.e. smart assistant devices or apps like Apple's Siri or Amazon's Alexa.

Evaluating How Business Leaders Make Use of Artificial Intelligence in Competing Against Each Other

A good idea is making use of the internet and so the relevant research concerning how other companies make use of AI technology for their advantage.

You can also read through your competitors' social media platforms and websites i.e. Facebook and LinkedIn. You can also browse their blogs, news coverage, and press releases. You can also look manually for annual reports or newsletters that may not be posted online.

You can cast the net wider and do a search i.e. how hotels using Artificial Intelligence, or even 'how companies are using Artificial Intelligence.

Researching on the manner in which additional components of your chain of supply and support make use of Artificial Intelligence. Don't forget to research about other avenues that are non-digital. If you're attending an event that is related to your industry, look out for Artificial Intelligence sessions. Go ahead and speak to people sitting or standing next to you. You could also read journals which will enable you to find out as much as you can about your competitors. Be sure to get information on how they make use of AI to their advantage. Always note down any useful information that can help you in the implementation of Artificial Intelligence in your business.

There are several types of Artificial Intelligence applications used in the business world but the most commonly applied one is the Machine Learning software. This particular application is basically tasked with processing huge data volumes, at a fast pace. This could also mean the reduction in the need for manual labour or even result in the over reliance of AI in performing various tasks in the business environment.

How to decide whether Artificial Intelligence will work for you in your Business

Several factors can act as your guideline when it comes to making the decision as to whether to make use of AI in your business. You need to have prior idea based on your findings concerning what AI has done for other companies. The companies you base your research on need to be in similar industry, and if possible, similar size.

Understanding that various tasks require certain data types to work will enable you to make better decisions on the AI system to acquire for your company. Make sure that you fully grasp the limits and requirements of the intended tasks.

Be sure to consider the types of process that can be carried out by Artificial Intelligence. This gives you an understanding of what AI will be utilized for, ensuring that the choice you make will yield positive results for your business.

Chapter 2 Is Artificial Intelligence a Blessing or a Threat in Business?

Technology is a very vital component in the growth and development of humans. AI is among these very vital technologies which are gaining hype and momentum. Technocrats have argued that AI can be a disaster and for some, a blessing.

The Core Benefits of Artificial Intelligence

As it will be seen throughout this guidebook, working with artificial intelligence comes with a lot of benefits. There are so many different industries that use this technology as well as so many different ways it can be utilized. With that in mind, we have to take a look at some of the various reasons why individuals, especially companies, would want to use this kind of technology to help them out.

Artificial intelligence is also fast and results in some quick actions, much faster than what we see with what a human or even a team of humans can do. Artificial intelligence can make decisions and work quickly. The brain of the machine, which is integrated with artificial intelligence, takes actions so quick that it can help to provide you with results in no time at all.

It also helps out in daily work. Are you already using Google Assistant? Do you work with Alexa and some of the other voice-activated assistants daily? Do you have a Smart Home and you have to speak to it to get things set at the way that you want? If any of these sound familiar to you, then you can already see how artificial intelligence can help you out in your daily work.

This is normal for most of us to deal with, but it can slow down work and productivity. When we work with an AI machine, we see that it does not get tired and it can work without all of the breaks. For many businesses, this can be good news. The machines that are integrated with artificial intelligence can work for a much longer duration of time at a high speed and a high amount of accuracy at the same time.

For the most part, these machines can reach much further than we would be able to do on our own. Due to a lot of the risk that comes with it, there are some places, and sometimes some circumstances, where humans cannot reach. Think about something like a fire, an important location for the military, and even some projects that take place out in space.

When these kinds of situations occur, rather than taking on too much risk along the way, a robot--one that has been programmed with artificial intelligence--would be able to complete the task and it can be done without any human interaction. Such a machine, if it is done and programmed correctly, can do the work and reach places where humans are more limited.

Using Artificial Intelligence decreases chances of making errors

These machines reduce error rates. When you use a machine that has artificial intelligence on it, we will see that the risk of error is lower compared to the work that humans do. This is one of the biggest advantages because it can save some industries millions of dollars. With the use the information that is already in artificial intelligence, along with some of the algorithms with it, the decisions for a company can be made quickly. The results are not only fast and easy, but the accuracy can be a lifesaver to a lot of different companies.

In most cases, decisions made by machines are greatly influenced by data that had been recorded previously hence the chances of any errors occurring is greatly reduced. This can be termed as a great achievement since problems solving can be handled without leaving room for errors, even for the complex ones.

Business establishments that are advanced prefer using digital assistants in the daily interactions with their viewers; this plays a key role in time saving. This also helps businesses in fulfilling the demands from their users without any delays. These systems have been programmed to deliver the best assistance possible to users.

Artificial Intelligence facilitates appropriate decision making

Machines have absolutely no emotions which makes it very easy for them to make decisions that are more efficient, within shorter time frames. This can be best outlined in the health sector. Integrating Artificial Intelligence in the healthcare facilities has greatly improved efficiency in the administration of treatments. This is through the minimization of the occurrences of inappropriate diagnosis.

Artificial intelligence machines are better at assisting than humans. These kinds of assistants can make much better decisions without adding in the emotions and biases we see with humans. Sometimes, these emotions and biases are good for us and can help with decisions, but often, they get in the way and they will cause us to make poor decisions along the way. This becomes less of a problem when we work with artificial intelligence.

Since the artificial intelligence machine does not have to work with these emotions, they can work efficiently without having any personal issues in the process. Besides, when we look at how this technology is used as a chat bot, we see that they are designed to chat about the problems that will help a human find their solution, and nothing else, so the emotions are kept to a minimum.

Artificial Intelligence can be used in risky instances

There are some instances where safety for human beings becomes vulnerable. i.e. survival for human beings on ocean floors is very difficult. Machines that have been fixed with algorithms that are predefined are used in studying these ocean floors. This is a major limitation that Artificial Intelligence has assisted to overcome.

Machines have the capability of working continuously

Working without brakes is another benefit that you get with AI. As a regular person, we need to take a break after we do so much work. We all get tired; our brains are not designed to work 24/7 all the time without any breaks. We need time away from work, a break, and some time to relax and do what we want and what we enjoy rather than working all of the time.

Unlike human beings, machines don't suffer from fatigue, even after working for many hours. This is a huge advantage over humans; they require time to rest for them to work efficiently. However, the efficacy of machines isn't determined by external factors. This means that these external factors don't reduce the working efficiency of machines.

Another benefit is the utility there is for society. You need to understand the value of chat bots. These are helpful because they can listen to a voice command, then it will go through and translate it for someone who does not know that particular language but who would still like to talk.

This is just one example of how the artificial intelligence can help out the society. Another one is with the idea of a self-driving car, which you can use to reach the location that you want, with better road safety and no crashes in the process.

And finally, we can look at how the idea of artificial intelligence can benefit us with some of the possible future innovations. Right now, one example of using this kind of technology is with Google AI, which is already looking at how it can be implemented in Biosciences and Healthcare. Recently, you may have heard about how this process will be able to detect things like diabetes by determining the retina depth. And if it is used properly, it can find more common diseases in humans and help us to get more benefits for our health in the process.

The Disadvantages of Artificial Intelligence

While artificial intelligence has a lot of benefits, and it seems like more and more people and businesses are coming on board with this kind of technology and trying to use it for their needs, some disadvantages come with this process as well. It is not always as positive as you may think, and while a lot of companies decide to use it for their needs and to help them grow and provide better customer service for their customers, there are some times when it is not the best decision for you.

What are these disadvantages? And how can you tell whether using artificial intelligence is the right option for you? Below are some of the disadvantages that you can watch out for, and at least consider, when it comes to the growth of artificial intelligence and using AI in your business.

Artificial intelligence can be too expensive. One of the biggest problems and one of the main reasons why people choose to not use this in their business is that constructing a system or a machine that uses this technology can be expensive. Think about how much work needs to be done in this process to make things work and how much it will cost to have enough power, to make the algorithm, to sort through the data, and more. For some big businesses, this cost makes sense and can save them money. But for some of the smaller companies, the cost is just going to be too big and they will forgo using this process.

Because AI-integrated machines are very complex, they cost more to maintain and use. In addition to this, they also cost a lot to keep the system up and running as well as the repair. Artificial intelligence is relatively new right now, which means that these machines, even though they may be relatively new, have to be updated constantly with the changing technology.

When totaling the repair, maintenance and installation costs of Artificial Intelligence, the proposition is clearly very expensive. This isn't viable for industries and businesses that don't have sufficient funds; it proves very difficult for the implementation of AI technology into the businesses' strategies or processes.

Next is that they do not have any emotions. Sometimes, this is a good thing, but other times, it does leave something out that we need as well. Humans are emotional and highly sensitive, which is what makes us human. This is something that we have been able to get from nature and makes us unique and who we are.

Instead of having emotions to help guide it, artificial intelligence relies on coding and programming. Deciding in some circumstances does not work with these programs, and sometimes, it is based on emotions. You will not be able to do this the right way with artificial intelligence, and that can mean that some decisions are not made correctly.

The artificial intelligence machine does not have any continuous self-development. A lot of times, humans learn a lot from the time they are children up until they are adults and so on. This is natural with humans and it means that they can learn and self-develop at the same time from the experiences that they had in the past. But this is not something that we see with artificial intelligence; it does not have any experience really, but will be based on the programming it has been given.

The machine only has a chance to "learn" something new if we take the time to update the program.

The AI machine does not have any innovation by itself. As we take a look at humans, we can see throughout the years that they have always been creative. This is a gift that we have been given by nature, and all of us have different levels of creativity. Some of us are creative with writing, some with drawing, some with music, some with coding, and so on. Each of us has a different type of creativity, but as a whole, humans are born with some kind of creativity, and this is the basis of our developing world right now.

But, think about a machine. Does that machine can do something brand new and be creative on its own without the programmer? Artificial intelligence, at least now, has not been built to handle this kind of process. It can help us in a lot of different ways. It can be useful for businesses and the customers in many cases. But for now, at least, it cannot handle anything like creativity and innovation all on its own.

Using the Artificial Intelligence has greatly increased the reliance on machines. Human beings have become increased dependent on machines. In the coming times, it might get to a point where it will be impossible for human beings to perform their duties without the aid of machines. The dependency of human beings on machines is bound to increase in future. This will result in the cognitive capabilities of human beings decreasing with time.

Machines Fitted with Artificial Intelligence perform restricted tasks. These machines have been programmed to perform certain duties with regards to what they have been programmed and trained to do. Relying on these machines in instances that may require the adaptation to unfamiliar environments can be frustrating. Machines don't possess the ability to think in a creative manner since their reasoning is restricted around the specific areas they have been programmed to do.

The last disadvantage would be the idea of human replacement. The machine that uses artificial intelligence can indeed help us out in many ways and sometimes do things that are not within the reach of us as humans. But it can never completely replace what a human can do.

People have been displaced from manual jobs. This is the main worry for technocrats. There is the possibility that Artificial Intelligence will end up displacing several low skilled workers. Machines have the ability to work non-stop which has resulted in companies preferring to use machines instead of using manual labour. The world is edging towards automation which will mainly result in the majority of jobs being carried out by machines i.e. in the scenario where there is the inception of the driverless cars, uncountable drivers have been pushed into unemployment.

This is beneficial in many ways because it ensures that we can all still have our jobs in the future. But it can have some issues in industries that face shortages with enough employees to help get the work done regularly. While we can take artificial intelligence and get it to do a lot of neat tasks for us and help to pick up the slack, it is not human, and there will be some glaring aspects that show up with this over time.

This is just one of the ways that artificial intelligence can help us benefit society. This technology is just getting started, and we are likely going to see it grow and change more over time. But we need to make sure that we are aware of some of the disadvantages and not just focus on the benefits, or we will miss out on some of the important parts of AI.

In conclusion, rather than replacing human ingenuity and intelligence, Artificial Intelligence is generally viewed as a subsidiary tool.

Irrespective of the fact that Artificial Intelligence is finding it hard to complete obvious tasks presently, it's skilled in analyzing and processing volumes of data quicker than the human brain. This is a good thing in relation to the business world in the sense that AI accelerates the rate at which tasks are carried out, saving time that can greatly be reflected in increased sales.

When it comes to making the decision about whether to make use of Artificial Intelligence applications in your business or not, always evaluate whether the AI will work for the good of the business or vice versa. Always make considerations about the cost implications as well as other factors like if the systems will have any impact in profits maximization. Will Artificial Intelligence help you in making informed decisions? Will the AI lead to rendering people who have worked for you for decades jobless? What impact will the same have in their livelihoods? These questions are important when making informed choices as you take the next step in installing AI systems in your business.

Chapter 3 The Important Ethics Highlighted in Artificial Intelligence

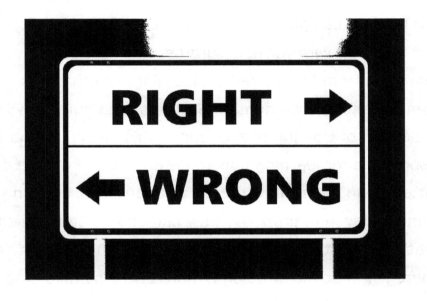

When it comes to working with artificial intelligence, there are also a few ethical considerations that we need to take into account. It is strange to think that working with a machine brings up some ethical concerns, but it is something that we need to be careful about. Machines may not learn the information the way that they should or they may also make mistakes, so it is important to consider some of the ethical points that can come with it.

First, we need to be careful about artificial stupidity, and how we can guard against some of the mistakes that come up with these programs. Intelligence emanates from the process of learning, whether it is from a machine or a human. Systems are equipped with some kind of training phase, and in this phase, they are responsible for learning how to determine the correct patterns, and learn how they are supposed to act. On training a system properly, they can enter into the next phase, the testing phase, which involves the process where it will be hit with some more of the sample data to see how well it will perform.

Of course, our training phase, while it can be pretty complete, cannot go through and cover all of the possible examples for the system. There will be times in real world situations when the input is something new, something that the system did not see during the training and the testing phase. The said systems may, at given times, be fooled in manner that a human would not be fooled.

For example, machine may "see" some things that are not there when it comes to a random dot pattern. If we decide to rely on artificial intelligence all the time to set us into the appropriate efficiency, security, and labor, we have to be certain that the machine works in the correct manner as planned, and it can be hard to catch when these mistakes are happening and how they are going to influence our decisions and how things happen.

Another issue is when it comes to being neutral and fair. Sure, it can add in a lot of speed, and the capabilities it has for processing is much more than what humans can do, but sometimes, it is not seen as neutral or fair.

A good example of this is Google Photos. AI is utilized to aid in identifying people in the pictures, scenes, and the objects. It can do a great job, but sometimes, it can be incorrect like when the camera issues the mark and on being sensitive racially. Sometimes, when the software used to help law enforcement to predict who will be a future criminal, there is often a bias shown for black humans.

We have to always remember that, with things like this, AI systems were molded by humans, and these humans tend to be judgmental and biased on occasion. If it is used correctly or by someone who is trying to reach social progress, AI is considered a catalyst to bring about some positive change.

Sometimes, security can also be an issue. We may think that using this kind of technology will help us do well in protecting against fraud, doing facial recognition, and more, but these systems can be corrupted as well. It is often a question of how AI can be kept safe and secure from those who want to get on and cause some problems along the way.

The more power we see with technology, the more that this technology can be used for not only good reasons but also for dangerous reasons. This can even include some of the systems that are prone to bringing about damage if they are maliciously used. This can cause some issues with cyber security and how safe you are when you do some work online or when you use some of your personal information.

We also have to take some time to look at the idea of singularity and how people are meant to stay in control of some of the complex intelligent systems that become popular when we move into the future. This can bring up the questions of whether the machines can become the fastest, strongest, and most intelligent things out there.

While most people realize that the machines and systems that rely on artificial intelligence are more as tools that we can control, there are some of those who bring up the ethical concerns that this process can someday try to work independently of humans, and it will be hard to control what is going on with the system and stop it from causing problems.

Of course, most of the worries that come with this kind of thing are movies and sci-fi stuff and not really something that we need to worry about when it comes to this process. The machine is meant to do what the code says and will not interact with the world in any way than it is set up to do. If it is set up to work as a search engine, it finds the results to search queries. It will not have emotions or view the world and do things in any other manner than how it relates to that job.

And this is the same no matter what kind of system you are using with artificial intelligence. It can be smart and intelligent, but only where it is designed for. Anything outside of this is not in the capabilities of the machine, so the machine going out of control is kind of silly to think about. If the program is not working well, then it just needs to be turned off and not used any longer.

Another concern is how machines can affect our human interactions and behaviors. There has been a rise in bots that are artificially intelligent and becoming so much better when it comes to modeling the kind of relationships and conversations that humans have regularly. They will not have the emotions or the same meaning behind them as humans do, but they can model this pretty convincingly along the way.

During the Turing Challenge in the year 2015, it surprised many when a bot given the name Eugene Goostman was declared the winner. This was the first ever win for the bot. In the challenge, the human raters would utilize text input to facilitate a chat with a given entity they did not know, and then they would stop and guess whether they had spent their time chatting with either a machine or a human. Eugene Goostman was able to fool over half the number of human raters, and many of them left thinking that their chatting session was with a human, rather than with a machine.

This success-point is just the beginning of an era where people may learn how to interrelate with machines just the same way we react with other humans. This could be seen in our regular lives someday, but often it is seen more in things like sales or customer service. While human beings have a limitation in the levels of kindness and attention they can give on someone else-- all of us have our bad days where we are not going to have the best day--artificial bots have the capability of stepping in and channel in resources that are virtually unlimited to help build up the relationships that they need.

Even though we may not realize it, humans are already seeing a time when these machines are capable of triggering the right reward centers within the brain of an individual. Think about video games and clickbait headlines. Such headlines are highly enhanced with the use of AB testing, which is a beginner type content optimization using algorithmic tricks that has the main goal of capturing our attention. Together with some other methods, is used to help make mobile games and videos more addictive.

But, is this necessarily a good thing? It often depends on how technology is used. If it is causing addiction and just lining the pockets of a big corporation and harming the customer in the process, then it is a bad thing. If we can harness the software for something good and use it correctly to help nudge society as a whole towards behavior, that is more beneficial overall, then it can definitely be a good thing.

Many good things can be seen with this kind of technology, but the reason for it being developed and the minds behind it determine whether it is used for good or for something bad. Finding a way to monitor how the algorithms are being used and to make sure that technology is used to help people to progress society and not for something more manipulative.

Another concern that some experts have, in specific, when we start to work more with machine learning, is the reward versus punishment as well as the near future ramifications that come with artificial intelligence. Some of the most intriguing of the research is already happening right now, and we need to be on the lookout for how this will shape our world. The two areas where the near future ramifications can already happen will include with reinforcement learning, which deals with punishment and rewards rather than with labeled data, and GAN, or generative adversarial networks, which allows the algorithms for a computer to create things rather than merely assess by having two nets compete against one another.

We can see the first one with Google DeepMind's Alpha Go Zero, while the second one can be seen by original audio or image generation based on learning about a certain subject, such as a specific type of music or like celebrities to name a few examples.

We can take this to a much larger scale. Artificial intelligence is already set up to have a lot of effects when it comes to environmental issues, climate change, and sustainability. Ideally, and partly with the help of more sophisticated sensors, cities reduce some of their congestion. They will have less pollution and will become more livable in the process.

Once you can predict something like this, it is possible to go through and prescribe certain rules and policies in the process. The sensors that are found on cars, the ones that can send in data about the conditions of traffic on that road and at that time, could later be used to predict some of the potential problems that will come up so that the flow of cars is optimized all on its own. Yes, this process is not really in use yet, and it is not perfect. It is just in the beginning stages, and the algorithms are just starting to learn. But, in the future, the algorithm will have time to take in more data and learn, and it will not be long until this plays a big role.

We have to consider also artificial intelligence and how it affects our human rights and our own privacy. A lot of people have been making a fuss about how artificial intelligence relies on big data which is already impacting privacy in a big way. Two examples of this are the eavesdropping that comes with Alexa from Amazon and the issues with Facebook and its Cambridge Analytica. These are just two of the examples of this kind of technology going wild.

Without the right kind of regulations being put into place and with self-imposed limitations in the process, many critics argue that this kind of thing becomes really common, and we are sure to see this get worse.

Many people agree that, when this kind of technology is used properly, then it can improve and benefit our society. But when no one looks after the technology and making sure that it behaves properly, then this is when problems come in.

Companies and entities that choose to work with artificial intelligence need to be smart about the work they are doing with it. They cannot just allow it to collect a lot of information and use it in any way that it "learns" how to do. This puts a lot of people at risk and it can allow those who control it or those who are able to get access to the information the ability to hold onto things that should be private.

Both of these issues bring up the idea that we need to be careful about how artificial intelligence is being used and how we can program it. It is not always as easy as it seems, and being smart and intelligent about it, rather than lazy, can help to get the full utilization out of the technology.

As we can see, a lot of different sides come up when we talk about artificial intelligence--the good side, the benefits, and some of the many reasons why you would want to start using artificial intelligence in your daily life and to help your business to grow. There are disadvantages, which can explain why not every person or business jumps on board and use this technology all of the time. And then, there are some ethical considerations that we need to pay attention to as well.

Artificial intelligence is taking over many aspects of our world; it is likely to grow more into the future as well. Having a good understanding of how this can work and all of the different parts that come together with this can be so important when it comes to helping us understand what artificial intelligence is, what it is not, and what we can expect as it comes with us into the future.

Chapter 4 How AI is Transforming Industries

Two engineering students founded the company Research in Motion in 1985. This company developed the famous BlackBerry device, which was the precursor of the smartphone. In the late 90s and early 2000s, Research in Motion was one of the most valuable technology companies in the world. Now, it's well past its heyday.

Change is not a question of if, but when. Even the largest companies can change or disappear. So can whole civilizations and superpowers. You too should expect change. Change in the business world can be driven by shifts in customer expectations, the invention of new and disruptive technologies, new competitors, and more. As you think about your own work ecosystem, it is important to understand what changes are happening.

Given the breadth of possibilities, in this book we are going to only discuss the changes driven by disruptive technologies. Again, technology is just one factor that you can model in order to better understand change. You could extend the modeling to include other drivers of change as well, and that should become clear by the time you finish the book.

How Is AI Changing Agriculture?

AI will also change agriculture. Did you know, for instance, that AI can monitor and predict the quality of flowers and plants in real-time? The core is a software module for quality prediction, in which influential factors on the quality of flowers and their expected effect have been mapped. Data obtained from sensors can supplement the predictions. The calculation rules from the model are always refined based on this data, thereby improving the reliability of the forecast. There is also an AI robot system that can sort and can detect potato diseases. The system is able to detect, identify, and quantify many of the common areas that affect potatoes. Also, greenhouse decision support systems are designed with AI. These systems make it possible to predict the environmental conditions that affect the growth and productivity of plants, and to adjust the temperature fluctuation. There are even AI-systems that have the ability of prescribing feed rations, medicines, health, and general welfare for cattle. This one might seem strange, but the system can also suggest best mating partners that will ensure the offspring has improved genetic potential.

Although majority of features are a work in progress, it's fantastic to see the vast number of opportunities AI brings about in all kinds of industries. In the next chapter, we'll take a closer look at how you can work with AI.

Technology Driving Change

Technology is evolving at a fast pace. You may remember the rise and fall of Pokémon Go in 2016, which was but a blip on the timescale. Few are talking about it now, but for several months the game was disrupting normal life.

A few decades ago, nobody anticipated some of the business models of today. Uber threatens to overshadow the rest of the taxi market and yet it owns very few cars. Airbnb has more room listings than the largest hotel chains and yet it owns very few properties.

Netflix is the largest TV streaming service and yet it owns no theaters. Netflix leveraged a better business model to put Blockbuster out of business. Facebook is the largest content sharing company and yet it produces little original content.

Applications like Spotify and products like Roomba are using technology to establish new business models. Pokémon Go did too, but quickly disappeared. The old notion of "first define the business, then figure out the technologies to enable that business" is not applicable anymore. Tomorrow's business models will be created based on the technology that is available then.

Now when a new technology emerges people figure out how to implement it in new business models. We have seen this time and time again. Without the internet, Amazon would not have been conceived of, much less thrived. Without the smartphone, Uber would not have been possible.

New business models have been born, not of a single technology but of an intelligent interweaving of multiple technologies. These technologies include cloud computing, social networks, IoT, mobile devices, AI, blockchain, and virtual reality (VR), among others. Using innovative business models, new entrants to the market are posing a severe threat to incumbents, many of which have been too slow to adjust. These newer companies are doing the equivalent of unbundling the monolithic companies—in other words, breaking up the functions of the larger companies into smaller units that can be rearranged in innovative ways. Likewise, many new and disruptive technologies will be integrated into new companies and coexist with old and yet-to-be-invented technologies. This is another example of super convergence.

Technology permeates business today; the two are tightly integrated. In fact, the lines between business and technology are becoming blurry. Because technology is so integral to business, leaders must know how to leverage it in their organizations. They need to understand what any given technology can or cannot do; how it works; how it can be combined with other technologies; what its impact is on the other elements of the organization such as processes, people, and data; how competitors may leverage it to their advantage; and how to integrate it into the organization.

Let's look a little deeper into the implications of AI. What happens if a new business model emerges in the same industry and space that your company operates in? This business won't have to worry about the cultural mindset or the legacy systems and processes in place. While your company may have experience and deep knowledge of the domain, the new company can make a clean start. As with anything, knowledge becomes outdated over time. To compete effectively, many elements of your company may have to be adjusted— elements like culture, systems, processes, and business models. If you can identify the elements of your business that have to be modified and develop a plan for change, you will have a fighting chance.

Some business models such as those of Amazon and Google are entirely based on technology—if you took away the technology, there would be no business. Companies such as Airbnb and Uber would not exist if the technology to facilitate their transactions were not available. Some companies like Southwest Airlines, on the other hand, use technology—particularly the internet—to enhance their existing business models and adapt along the way. Southwest Airlines started with the only relevant technology available at the time: the telephone. Then it adapted to the internet and mobile devices.

Borders bookstore had physical locations that cost a lot of money to maintain. Expenses included rent, utilities, customer-facing employees, etc.—something Amazon did not have. Amazon, which commenced as an online bookseller, displaced Borders bookstores because it used technology effectively in a new business model. Amazon could stock a much larger inventory in its warehouses since it did not have multiple retail locations. It saved on retail costs and could pass those savings on to customers. It developed an efficient distribution and shipping system. It did not have to train customer-facing employees. It tracked purchase patterns on a near-real-time basis and responded accordingly. Analytics were built into its operations from the ground up, which enabled Amazon to react quickly to changing market conditions.

Circuit City was another company that fell victim to Amazon. The money and resources invested in its physical stores was hard to recoup.

Amazon continues to disrupt not only other companies, but also itself. Many times Amazon cannibalizes its own business, such as when it allows other merchants to sell on its website (unlike its competitors like Walmart). Its website becomes a transaction medium rather than an online retail store, in which case it makes less profit per sale. Nonetheless, it seems to have successfully built a culture around the philosophy of, "If you are not moving forward, you are moving backward."

Uber is undoubtedly a unicorn—which happened to come up with a great business model. With this model, potentially every car becomes a cab. This completely upsets the business model of traditional cab companies. On top of this, Uber is experimenting with self-driving cars. When this becomes practically feasible in the next few years, the company can essentially be run with few people and a lot of software. While Uber is an extreme example, it is a realistic one and proves the point that tomorrow's organizations have the potential to run services primarily with machines and software instead of humans.

A few years back, travel agents used to help coordinate travel plans for customers. With the World Wide Web, online travel sites started displacing travel agencies, as customers could explore and find deals themselves. Low prices and better control over purchases are a strong attraction for customers and difficult to compete with.

When a certain product or service shifts to be a commodity, it is easier to standardize it and offer it over the web. This puts power in the hands of the customers. Customers also like uniqueness and don't always choose the standard commoditized product or service. In an earlier time, we would have hired more people to help with the customization. However, now we have a new technology—AI—that can help with that.

Tesla is able to offer cars directly to its customers by leveraging the internet, whereas legacy auto companies such as GM and Ford are forced to sell their cars through dealers. As you can imagine, it is difficult to change that business model by taking dealers out of the equation. Because Tesla has a direct relationship with its customers with no go-betweens, it can understand their behaviors and expectations faster and adapt quickly, while saving the cost of the intermediaries. In fact, it is able to send direct software updates to its cars wirelessly to identify and fix problems. Tesla has gathered over 1.2 million miles of autopilot data, which if harnessed correctly can offer a huge competitive advantage.

For yet another example, consider insurance. Like travel agencies, insurance companies with their vested agent model are at risk. Traditional insurance providers sell through their agents, but newer business models like Lemonade sell directly to the customer. The sale and service of simple products like auto insurance can be done by automated systems, and the sale and service of complex products like life and health insurance can be done with the help of AI systems. Agents will have to invest in enhancing a different set of complementary skills, such as building deeper relationships with customers and empathizing with them in cases of loss. You might think that insurance is a complicated product, but with technologies like AI, machines may eventually be able to do most of the work. Then what happens?

As more technology becomes available, more business models are possible. In the future, even more advanced technologies may supersede the current business models of Amazon and Facebook.

Having given some examples of how technology drives change, I'd like to emphasize that technology by itself is not the only factor. Technology exists within the context of a whole system, and some parts of the system may have to change to accommodate the technology. In this battle, sometimes technology loses, or at least its adoption is postponed.

Other factors in the system may deter change, and the best technology does not always win. This is due to the strength of the underlying system and the network that a company could be a part of. In the case of GM, its distributers are going to fight tooth and nail to keep their business models. Social and political battles will have to be fought and won before direct relationships with customers will become more common for traditional automobile companies.

As another example, consider the U.S. tax system. Transitioning to a flat tax system would be extremely difficult, because there are so many parties that form an integral part of the current system and have a strong vested interest in it. These parties include accountants, tax consultants, tax software creators, and even the IRS. A lot of people could potentially lose their jobs if the U.S. transitions to a flat tax system. In this hypothetical example, even though we have the technology to change, the overall system may resist.

New, nimbler companies with AI-based business models will threaten the incumbents. AI technologies will give rise to new business models. A company may have the best employees, but if the underlying business model is flawed, the company stands no chance of survival.

As another example, consider typewriters, which have virtually disappeared. Even if you hire the best salespeople to sell typewriters, you will not succeed. That's why the business model is an important element to consider in evaluating an ecosystem.

AI is driving change in business. The ingredients of AI— availability of large amounts of data (or big data), high computing power in the form of GPUs (graphical processing units) and TPUs (tensor processing units), and advanced machine learning algorithms—make it easier for businesses to change and transform themselves. Cloud and technology vendors are offering AI expertise in the form of services that businesses can leverage in their transformation. All the components to enable successful digital transformation are falling into place. This is why the time for AI is now!

Challenges to Integrating Technology into Business

Years before the smartphone, Apple came up with the Newton, which was a handheld device intended to track your calendar, appointments, and notes. By today's standards it was rudimentary, but at the time, the technology was at the cutting edge. The technology itself might have been accepted, but after a well-known cartoonist derided it for being an overpriced paper notebook and Steve Jobs made his distaste of it known, the project was terminated. Factors other than technology caused its rejection in the marketplace. This again shows that the integration of technology into an organization is not only a technological issue. Rather, it requires changes along multiple dimensions such as social acceptance, organizational structure, business processes, vendor relationships, and employee functions.

When the iPhone was released years later, it gained wide acceptance quickly, primarily due to two reasons: (1) people had been exposed to new forms of digital technology by that time and were ready and (2) the technology had improved so much that there was less friction and more ease of use. Making the best use of this acceptance by users, Apple was able to build a full ecosystem of connections among its devices and applications—like the iMac, Apple Watch, iTunes, etc.

Many new and disruptive technologies are continuing to emerge. These or combinations of these will be harnessed in new business models. Let's look at some of the potential challenges.

Integrating these technologies into an existing business model is a herculean task. When integrating technologies, it's necessary to think about the future: what is going to happen ten or twenty years from now.

One of the best approaches is to start from scratch, but most companies do not have that option or flexibility. Only a few companies, such as Google, are able to pull it off. The existing context and ecosystem have to be considered, and we have to work within those constraints.

The viable alternative is to understand your existing industry to the extent that you can figure out how to effectively adjust to super convergence of the technology and transformation of your business. This requires an engineering approach to designing your own future. The principles of such an engineering approach are what I will discuss in the later chapters, with a specific focus on the integration of AI.

Adjusting to AI

Many of the ways businesses operate will change in the next five years, and we have to adapt now.

As I mentioned earlier, we will be inundated by data as the volume of information continues to grow quickly. AI will be the ideal technology to consume this data and "learn" from it. For this reason, it will become an integral part of most organizations. As most businesses' processes are infused with some form of AI, they will undergo massive disruption. But, just like we have gotten used to technologies such as computers and the internet, we will get used to AI.

Many business processes will have intelligence built into them so as to react to a dynamic ecosystem and varying customer needs. Traditionally, categories of customers were segmented into large groups. Now, with the power of data and intelligence, customers are increasingly being treated and catered to as individuals. Organizations and their processes are being driven to be nimble and adapt to each customer's unique needs.

Humans and machines will be collaborating at new levels, complementing their respective strengths to solve big problems. Businesses will need to construct the ecosystem that makes this collaboration possible. To construct such an ecosystem, they must first understand everything that needs to be in it.

If you were planning a camping trip, you'd list the things that you would have to pack—tent, sleeping bags, stove, etc.—depending on a number of internal and external factors, such as how far the camping site was from a grocery store, what the weather was going to be like, how much water you would need to store, whether you would have to worry about wild animals, and so on.

This is essentially similar to planning for the business ecosystem, but there are a few differences. One is scale. A business is much larger than a campsite. Another is coordinating decision-making responsibilities among multiple people. If one person or group of people were responsible for providing the "tent" and another the "pegs," you would want to make sure that the pegs were suitable for the type of tent procured. In the real world, this is a bigger challenge than you'd think. There is no "enterprise checklist" that's comparable to a camping list. As you can see, the more "stuff" and constraints you add, the bigger the challenge—but it can be done.

To summarize, technology is driving fundamental changes in business. In fact, it is difficult to find a business today that in some way is not driven by technology. Businesses will continue to leverage technology for their operations and competitive advantage. If you want to adapt to and thrive in the business environment of the future, you need to understand how technology, and especially AI, can impact your life.

Chapter 5 How AI is Improving Healthcare

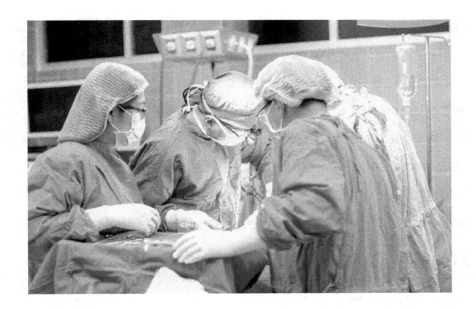

Another area where AI can change the world is in the medical field. It is working to improve and make work more efficient in the medical field in a lot of different ways, and as more advances in this kind of technology become more common, it is likely to that we will see it even more than before. This is good news for those who are looking to get into the medical field or those who want to ensure that their quality of life keeps going up in the process as well.

There are a lot of ways that AI can help out with various parts of the medical world, even if we may not realize it right now. Being on the outside, looking in, it may seem like we are not seeing much of this. But often, a lot of the procedures and results you get from the doctor will be given thanks to some of the AI technology. With this in mind, let us take a look at some of the ways that AI has already made an influence on the medical field!

Analyzing Images

Right now, many of the providers you visit see many different images at a time. The provider has to stop throughout their day and look at images of the brain, X-rays of all kinds, ultrasounds, and so much more to help them see what is wrong with their patient. And each patient may need this kind of imaging done, though it is not as likely that everyone will need this. But if the doctor has 50 patients, and half of them need some kind of imaging done during that visit, then the doctor has a lot of information to look over and make a diagnosis from.

But, maybe, it does not need to be this way. It is possible that with the help of AI, the provider would be able to work with a machine to help look over the images and come out with a good diagnosis in just a few minutes, and sometimes faster, rather than the provider having to do all of the work themselves and possibly making mistakes along the way. This is exactly what a team in MIT is working on. They have been able to work with a machine learning algorithm that can look at scans and then give an analysis in a much faster and more efficient way than the provider can do on their own.

Of course, this process is not meant to replace what the doctor can do, but it is there to help make the doctor more efficient. Rather than spending 15 minutes on 25 patients, these images can be done and analyzed in just a matter of minutes, and the doctor can spend more time with their patients and on other things rather than just trying to take a look at the images all of the time.

In addition to this, it is also the hope that AI can help to improve some of the newer radiology tools that will be released, ones that will be able to help with diagnoses without needing to rely on samples of tissue all of the time. These AI image analyses would be able to be useful in more remote areas, the ones that may not be able to reach as many medical devices or have the same kinds of doctors that those in larger areas would as well.

The most exciting part is that it can make healthcare more available to everyone. Telemedicine, when it is used properly with AI systems, will become more effective because patients--no matter where they are located--will be able to use the camera on their phone to send in pictures of things like cuts, rashes, bruises, and more so they can determine if care is really needed, freeing up the resources of the hospital and saving time for minor things and do not really need to be seen by a doctor.

Surgery Assisted by AI

Another healthcare industry benefit is the use of AI to assist with some kinds of surgery. With a value that is estimated to be somewhere near $40 billion in the healthcare industry, robots can take some of the available data from medical records and use this information to guide the instrument that the surgeon is using at the time. This can help to make the surgery more effective, reduce the amount of time the patient stays in the hospital up to 21%, and so much more.

While this may seem a little bit scary to have a computer work on your surgery, it has quite a few benefits. First, it is not as invasive as some of the other surgery types out there, and this helps to keep the scar smaller and improves the healing time. At the same time, the robot can gather up data on other operations similar in the past, and then will tell the surgeon about any new surgical technique that they could use as well. The results at this time may still be newer, but they are positive and promising.

In one study, a tally of 379 was picked for orthopedic patients. It was found that when they underwent an AI-assisted procedure, they had fewer complications going to five times lower as compared to those who just had the surgeon do the operation on their own. In another study for the first time ever, there was choosing of a robot to do eye surgery, and the best developed robot for surgical purposes, the Da Vinci, which allows the doctor to go through procedures that are pretty complex with high levels of control compared to some of the approaches that are used on regularly.

Another example of how these AI-assisted surgery robots can help is in the case of Heartlander, a tiny robot used to help out heart surgeons. This little robot can enter into a smaller incision that the surgeon puts into the chest to undertake both mapping and some therapy measures on the hearts surface. This helps to make heart surgery less invasive, more efficient, and makes the patient heal and get better in no time.

Virtual Nursing Assistants

AI can also be used in the hospital to work with virtual nursing assistants. Starting from being able to interact positively with the patients who come in to directing the patient on where to go, you will find that these nursing assistants can be effective and could ensure the medical industry saves at least $29 billion a year, while helping to fill in some of the gaps that show up in this industry.

Since these kinds of nurses are present every day and all day long, this can make things easier for the patient as well. They can be there to answer any questions that come up, monitor how the patient is doing at different times, and even provide some quick answers without having to bring in a person to handle it. These can make them a lot more effective than what their human counterparts can be sometimes and will be helpful especially with hospital and clinic shifts that are short on staff.

Administrative Tasks

This kind of AI comes in use when you are working with the medical field and how the administrative part of this business will be able to interact with their customers. These types of machines would be set up in order to help all of the health care providers there, whether they are nurses, doctors or someone else, save more time to get their tasks done on a day-to-day basis as well, freeing them up to take care of the patients better, and ensuring that everyone gets their job done on time.

Technology, including transcriptions that go from voice conversion to text, could make it easier to order the tests that a patient needs, prescribe the right medications, and even write out the notes for charts for the doctor. When the doctor can get these things done more efficiently, without having to sit down and do them on their own or having to hire someone to follow them around to do it, then it saves a lot of time and money and makes for happier patients.

One example using the AI tools to help support administrative tasks is the known partnership that happened between IBM and Cleveland Clinic. This Clinic is currently working with Watson from IBM to undertake big data mining and to ensure that physicians can provide treatment experiences to their patients that are more efficient and personalized in the process.

One of the methods that the Watson program can support physicians is that it can take in a larger number of medical papers running into thousands with the help of NLP (natural language processing) and uses this information to help make treatment plans that are backed by research and are more informed than before.

As you can see, AI technology is can help the medical field out and can ensure that it will be as efficient as possible in many different ways. And we were just able to touch base on a few of the option! There is so much that is already being seen with AI in the medical field, and as more of this is developed, this is likely to become some of the norms as we move into the future.

Chapter 6 How Big Companies are Using AI

Exploiting the artificial intelligence of big companies can be the foundation upon which a business builds its presence in the marketplace. Some companies have experience in the AI industry spanning decades and are improving their platforms continuously with a target of growing their market share. These companies offer opportunities to smaller establishments to ride on their achievements as they move towards their strategic objectives. Small companies can choose a big organization aligning with their interests.

The advantages of exploiting AI of big companies are many, including the opportunity to create a competitive edge in the marketplace. These companies already are attracting brand loyalty and in extension can cause their clients to trust a small business seen to be sharing their AI system. When using the AI of big companies, small businesses may not have to worry about cybersecurity as much. The big companies are continuously looking for ways to protect their systems, therefore, having better protection than small businesses.

Big companies that have AI that small businesses can exploit are many with their platforms having different benefits that may assist small businesses. Some of the companies include Amazon, Apple, and Facebook. Another big company having AI that other organizations can exploit to their benefit is Google which has many AI products currently in the market. Each of the big companies produces AI platforms that are helping them in achieving their strategic objectives.

Google's Artificial Intelligence Activities

The artificial intelligence activities of Google are many with the company investing in continuously improving their AI capabilities which are in use across many businesses. These include Google Ads, Google Maps, and Google search engine, which companies are using worldwide. Each of these Google tools is providing varied benefits to those exploiting their capabilities within their contexts. Google's AI platforms are generally accessible online with different tools geared towards specific population segments. The abilities of Google AI-based activities depend on the generation and analysis of data. Machine learning and deep learning are capabilities of these AI platforms with new versions periodically released.

Google Ads is an AI activity for marketing and information purposes with the platform allowing businesses to create personalized ads. The delivery of these ads is dynamic with potential clients seeing them when they align with their changing interests. As potential customers are browsing through websites in affiliation with the Google company, they come across ads relevant to them. Currently, the AI capabilities regarding Google Ads are allowing for a suggestion of how to create ads making the process more convenient. The creative ad capability is allowing Google Ads to act as dynamic templates that businesses can exploit to further their interests.

Google Teachable machine is an AI that is for the student population, making it a platform that can expand the opportunity for businesses in the education industry. Companies looking to explore opportunities in understanding the concept of machine learning can find this AI useful. The teaching process has not integrated coding, which makes it easier to use for those inexperienced in computer languages. One uses a camera to aid the machine in learning with the lessons' facilitation being online-based. The platform is combining the advantages of AI and machine learning.

The Google Search engine may be the most recognizable AI from the company with businesses using the tool to source for information. The search engine uses algorithms that trigger answers to searches that come up when users type in keywords when looking for information. This AI platform can specify search results based on the location of the one typing the keyword giving greater information accuracy to businesses. Language-based results are possible, which creates a better customer experience for potential clients. Google search engine is now allowing users to translate pages that can create a connection with potential clients as they feel a part of the company.

Google Maps is an AI in use by businesses to augment their operations, for example, by the taxi-hailing apps available in the market. The drivers can use the AI to determine their location and the directions to where they intend to go, including tips like the shortest route. Google Maps are helping brick and mortar stores showcase their position, which may lead to an increase in walk-in clients. Companies can use Google Maps to increase customer interactivity by establishing tracking maps allowing customers to see the workflow of their transaction.

Regarding the AI technology by Google in use in search engines, businesses can use voice options to triggers searches to topics relevant to the organization. The Google AI of choice for companies can focus on needs the company is looking to fulfill both within and without the business entity. Businesses can employ varied Google AI platforms, consecutively. The Google AI possibilities are allowing for integrations with existing applications in use within organizations. There are specific Google AI applications geared towards assisting businesses to increase efficiency in various processes. The processes the AI tools may cover include marketing, sales, and operations.

Facebook's Artificial Intelligence Activities

The AI activities of Facebook can be thought to revolve around the underlying social nature of Facebook, taking into account the social changes. Businesses can use Facebook AI to track and report the dynamic changes within the society that may affect their operations. The follow up is via deep learning and machine learning with the details being of the highest quality. Facebook is generating purely social AIs that businesses can take advantage of the opportunities it presents. Facebook's AI activities involve more than one billion people giving their data a high level of data, and therefore higher levels of accuracy.

Facebook AI activities include analytics which businesses can use in understanding the interests of their clients and aligning their product and service offerings to their needs. The analytics Facebook shares are specific and dynamic as the data in use is continuously updated as people are interacting within their platform. Businesses can determine the parameters that they want to see, for example, filtered through location, age, and distance. Organizations are using the data from Facebook analytics to create new product and service offerings. The use can propel a business to a position of influence within the marketplace.

Chatbots are now available within Facebook for both personal and business pages with the latter helping organizations take advantage of the benefits of the AI tool. These are for messaging clients in a timely fashion using the automatic nature of AI-powered chatbots. The chatbots are in use by businesses for different purposes, for example, gathering of customer information. Chatbots by Facebook are in use by companies to upsell and market promotions to their potential client bases using the platform. Businesses are including links within the chatbots. These are leading customers to their websites, hoping to turn them from interested customers to actual clients.

Sponsored ads by Facebook is another form of AI businesses can take advantage of within the platform. These require payment by the organization after a set period. Companies are using ads to reach their intended target clients. The timing of the sponsored ads is possible, allowing a business to personalize their customer experience, which can be a source of the competitive edge in the marketplace. The types of ads companies can create through Facebook are different, including videos, and photos which can help a business reach visual customers. Facebook shares data on how the promotions are performing and allow changing of the content of the ads as they are running.

Facebook AI activities include running of survey questions within a user's newsfeed. The surveys are generally short containing one or two inquiries that require a click response which encourages a higher rate of customer action. Businesses can use this feature to get feedback from their potential customers regarding product and service offerings. The survey feature offers convenience as companies can create their own from their Facebook business pages. Businesses can create surveys in different forms, including poll questions. They can be versatile in terms of visual presentation, for example, including videos and pictures.

Facebook AI allows for third party integration of applications making it a versatile platform that businesses can align with their interests. These can be affiliated directly to Facebook like Instagram or not, for example, Survey Monkey. For Facebook affiliated programs, ad sharing is possible, which makes its use convenient. The integration can allow for smoother transition with applications already in use by businesses in various stages of their internal processes. It can save time for companies that have a presence across different social media platforms with their activities appearing on Facebook and other applications simultaneously.

Amazon's Artificial Intelligence Activities

The AI activities from Amazon are many with their focus being on continuous improvement of their systems that are giving them a competitive edge within the marketplace. The actions have grown it into a behemoth of online trading with a wide variety of products that potential customers have access to through their accounts. Amazon AI activities can benefit businesses of different sizes as their platform is versatile, allowing both digital and physical products. The actions have their basis in deep learning and machine learning which helps Amazon consistently improve on their offerings to potential clients. The developments are helping in breaking down barriers that were due to geographical limitations.

For physical products, Amazon has an AI-backed tracking system that allows customers to have real-time information on the location of their packages. The transparency has built their reputation as trustworthy, which is giving them a presence worldwide in terms of trade. Businesses can tap into this brand trust to move their items through the platform of Amazon around the world. Their experience with shipping is unmatched, which can save smaller businesses from dealing with the challenges that come with logistics. Companies can outsource tasks that Amazon can handle to focus on their core competencies, leveraging on their AI activities in the marketplace while achieving scale operations quicker.

The AI activities by Amazon span the world of payment processing with transaction confirmation occurring via automated email processing. The perception in the market of their ability to handle payments without fraud is positive enabling businesses to reach clients that trust its business model. Plugging into their robust system may mean growth for organizations as it exposes companies to new customer segments at a low cost. The AI activities at Amazon are allowing for cost calculation in a customer's local currency, making the transactions relatable. Businesses can, therefore, forecast their earnings in a currency that fits their local contexts.

Using AI, Amazon is allowing for the creation of personalized stores both for customers and for businesses which creates a better customer experience. One can control their purchasing or store collection conveniently with buying done from the comfort of one's home. Companies can lead potential customers to their storefronts within the Amazon platform at no extra costs to their business. Organizations can alter the outlook and feel of their digital storefronts conveniently with the touch of a button, which they can use to attain a competitive edge within the marketplace.

Amazon is using robots as part of their AI activity strategy. With the machines assisting the human workforce in varied business processes, they can achieve a quick turnaround time. Companies can leverage this advantage to reach customers faster while saving on costs. One of the areas where Amazon is integrating robots is within its warehouses to reduce errors and increase the speed of service. Businesses can use this strength to improve their customer experience, which may convert to increased market share. This investment is allowing Amazon to compete effectively with brick and mortar stores.

Amazon's innovation within the field of AI is allowing it to compete within the digital marketplace with the company creating its digital bookshop known as Amazon Kindle. Here, clients can access millions of books worldwide at the touch of a button which improves customer experience. Businesses can, therefore, go around the limitations of geographical barriers, which may increase their market reach. Uploading digital products is also convenient with individuals globally able to benefit from the technology. Amazon's AI activities, in this way, levels the field for businesses of smaller size to compete with the larger establishments.

Apple's Artificial Intelligence Activities

Apple's AI activities in the technology space are revolutionary with the company having a segment of customers who portray brand loyalty through their purchases. They run on the foundation of exclusivity with offerings of products and services available to those who select to purchase their devices. Data and machine learnings are part and parcel of the innovations within the company's portfolio of products.

Their segmentation of customers can be a market source for businesses looking to serve their exclusive club. Such companies will not have to bear the cost of segmentation as Apple takes on the same.

Apple, as a company, achieves exclusivity through the process of encryption. It does not allow non-affiliated systems to work with their products. The result is improved sales as customers have to keep updating their devices to remain in the exclusive club and the improved quality of services for their customers. The latter is through the passing of quality standards set by the company to be on their platform. Their customers also trust them giving them the advantage of brand loyalty that businesses can tap into to sell their products. Given the characteristics of their customer segments, organizations can tailor their product promotions to align with the interests of their clients.

Apple AI activities inform their sales strategy with precise segmentation, for example, aligning with expected income levels of potential customers. Apple devices are undergoing continuous improvement, establishing a perpetual sales cycle. Customers, will over time, update their devices through purchasing as changes reach a point of not being in tune with a tool. Businesses can align themselves with their sales strategy to come up with new product offerings that can be of interest to the customer segment within Apple's platform. The companies can improve their sales revenue while riding on the business model of the Apple company.

Apple AI activities come with challenges arising from their business model. Some are the attraction of those looking to hack into their system of exclusivity. There are scenarios where there are calls for the exclusivity to align with the political interests of societies. Some customers may not be able to keep up with the device changes in terms of purchasing, which cause a loss of customers. Due to geographical limitations, some customers may not access the latest innovations presented by the company to their client base. There has been a criticism of the company's ability to maintain a lead in AI innovation, given its model of exclusivity, which is an expectation of customers.

Apple, as a firm, operates the Apple store that holds different products, which may be of interest to their customer base. The products in the store must pass their standards to be part of the portfolio. Businesses can work to attain their requirements to sell their products and services to the customers, which may expand a company's market share. The exclusivity may work to the advantage of a company as customers may perceive a brand to be exclusive when associated with the Apple company.

The Apple company creates devices that are compatible with one another, and that cannot work with other third-party applications. Companies, depending on their strategic goals, can aim to have their devices work with the exclusivity of the Apple brand as a foray to new markets. Companies can focus on adjustability beyond the Apple Company. The effect could be achieving an extensive array of clients. Customers are now demanding products that are not restrictive which may be an opportunity for businesses. Versatility to a broader arena can mean working with more third-party applications as they would assume the products of a

company are of the level of the Apple Company
regarding the quality levels.

Chapter 7 Trends and Opportunities of AI in Business Applications

Email Marketing Optimization

Can AI increase open rates and leads across an email marketing campaign? The simple answer is: Yes, it can, but only in combination with other tech and factors. Phishing and spamming attacks lasting for over a decade force many consumers to not bother opening a single email that appears to be a marketing effort.

If you manage to increase email open rates by, say, 1 to 2 percent, it will generate billions in more sales globally. To do so you must achieve a level of personalization that only Big Data and AI can produce. You still need creativity that AI is unable to achieve at this stage but an AI-powered marketing software can tweak a core message to appeal to each particular consumer you are targeting via email.

Part of what makes artificial intelligence so powerful in business is that it is able to uncover aspects of business performance that were previously unknown. Although human beings are capable of recording data and interpreting it, AI (powered by computers) is capable of approaching information from a perspective that human beings often do not (or cannot). Deep learning has opened the door for AI agents to process data in complex ways, allowing businesses to use data in ways that they most likely would never have thought of before.

This is the idea of actionable analytics, one of the trends that will be discussed as the relationship between AI and business intelligence here. This particular trend hits at the heart of why applied artificial intelligence is so important. Most businesses have data that can be used to improve business performance and profitability, but they do not know how to use it, or they do not have the time or the brain power to be able to use this data effectively. Another potential problem is that businesses may not be keeping the data (or storing it properly) to allow them to improve their business competitiveness, a deficiency that would be quickly revealed when an information science or AI expert performed an analysis of a business's records.

If you are like most people, you may be suffering from a measure of information overload when it comes to artificial intelligence. Indeed, even if you have made it this far in the book, you still may be in the situation of feeling that the concepts of applied artificial intelligence still feel like something that you need help applying to your business. Frankly, this is kind of the point of AI. As long as your company's important data is stored in a way that AI can access it, the AI can do a lot of that analytical work for you. Think of AI as that super-smart MIT grad who you can bring into your company to figure out what your company needs to do to go from a small Mom and Pop shop to the next Amazon.

In short, the purpose of this chapter is to help applied artificial intelligence take a leap in your mind from the theoretical to the practical. The problem that many business owners have when they read books about AI is that their brain is filled with all of these sometimes confusing and overlapping ideas and they now have to figure out what all of this means for their business. Here we give you some of the trends in the area of AI and business intelligence to basically give your brain a break. These trends essentially are breaking down what AI can do for your business without you having to figure it out for yourself.

Trend 1. Ethical data practices increase in importance

The first trend that it is important to note in the area of AI and business intelligence has to do with the ethical use of data. This trend may come as a surprise to some, but it really should not. The modern world is bombarded with data that is being stored (often in secret) and accessed by people that governments, companies, and other responsible parties may not want to access that data. In other words, whenever you are dealing with data, you have to think about ethics. If you are a company that is keeping customer data, are you ensuring that the data is encrypted and secure? Who are you sharing the data with? Are you following the mandates of the law? Are you disclosing all of your practices to your customers?

Part of the problem here is that "data" and "information" have essentially taken on lives of their own. The law has not kept up to date with the ability of companies, government bodies, or whomever to access data. Indeed, the law in many jurisdictions often is not clear that governments have the right to store certain types of data on its citizens although we know that governments often do keep certain types of data and use it.

The law in places like the European Union and the United States has attempted to do a little bit of catchup here, but that still leaves a podium that business leaders need to step up to. General Data Protection Regulation (GDPR) in EU law attempts to give individuals more control over their personal data, partly in response to the revelation that large companies use the data of their customers or users in ways that the customers may not fully be conscious of.

What this means for you as a business leader is that you should be conscious that there is a drive for a code of ethics in data used by businesses. Businesses use data manipulated by AI technologies to make business decisions, but a particular business may not be aware of how precisely the data is being used and whether or not it is being used ethically. A business that does not put thought into ethical (and legal) use of data leaves itself open to being penalized by a government body or being edged out by a more ethical competitor.

Trend 2. Humanizing data with natural language

AI can take different forms. AI can be purely analytical in nature, taking on the cognitive abilities that were once the preserve of the brain, or it can approach human beings and "humanness" in various ways. Indeed, an idea mentioned in passing in this book is the way that the definition of artificial intelligence has changed to accommodate for the increasing roles (and increasing complexity) that has come to characterize AI as this type of technology has advanced. It is now assumed by some in computer science and information science worlds that artificial intelligence means the ability for machines to do things that human beings do.

The future of artificial intelligence, therefore, involves AI technology becoming more human in various ways. Although language processing as a capability has long been a part of the AI world, AI technology is becoming more sophisticated in its ability to understand and use language. Natural language processing (or NLP) represents the meeting point between computers and language. Computers are able to use NLP to analyze language data on a large scale, which, combined with machine learning, allows AI to become very sophisticated in terms of language understanding and application.

The idea of humanizing data is sometimes mentioned in the realm of business intelligence, and it really approaches the issue of AI and data from the perspective of the user or customer. If you think about large multinational companies like Google or Facebook, data is not merely something that the company stores and uses to improve its practices, it is a resource that is directly used by the customer. In other words, the customer interacts with the data almost as much as the company does.

Humanizing data with natural language, therefore, means making the experience of accessing data more natural and easy using AI. A business intelligence tool that is doing this effectively would, therefore, be able to understand a spoken request, no matter how out of the ordinary it is, and be able to provide the end user with the data that they seek. This humanizing data involves not only the understanding part, but the interpretation bit, and the response. An effective business intelligence tool would then be able to ask you a follow-up question to help clarify the data that is needed, much like how a human on the other end of a telephone might.

Trend 3. Explainable AI is becoming increasingly important

Automation is one of the key tools that artificial intelligence can lend to business. Automation is used not only to complete processes through machine learning, but it can also be used for decision-making. Because of machine learning, AI can reveal business insights that might have fallen under the radar previously. Again, this is a function of data and the ability of AI to use deep learning (a type of machine learning) to perform complicated analytical and predictive operations with data.

Explainable AI refers to the area of study that involves making artificial intelligence transparent and easily understandable to people. Of course, this raises the question of why it is necessary for complex AI technologies to be explainable, but some statistics can help shed light on the situation. It is predicted that by 2020, nearly 90% of Chief Information Officers at businesses will be involved with piloting AI programs at their companies. Making this technology explainable not only serves a role in the use of this technology, but it helps ensure that the technology serves the purpose that it is meant to serve.

Explainable AI is important for transparency, which is itself a trend in the realm of business intelligence and AI. Artificial intelligence technology is being used to make recommendations and to perform other predictive operations; in short, AI technology generates answers for people, whether these people are workers in the business performing their work duties or customers. Men and women working with AI need to be able to inquire about the information that AI technology generates.

Transparency allows those dealing with AI to understand what the AI is doing and whether the AI is working properly. Transparency also allows the company (and the technology) to establish a form of rapport with the client so that they are confident in the information that they are receiving from the AI. Explainable AI, therefore, allows business leaders and others to explain the answers that AI generates to clients and others, which will be increasingly important as AI technology becomes ubiquitous and more powerful.

Trend 4. Accelerated data movement to the cloud

Understanding data is essential to understanding how to implement AI technology into your company. You need to know where your data is, what format it is in, and how it is stored. Most readers are familiar with cloud storage, which has become an increasingly more common way for companies (and individuals) to store their data. Part of this is due to the cloud-based technology that some companies like Google and Adobe promote, while some of this change also has to do with the power of the cloud and how the cloud can work with AI.

Sure, some have personal opinions about cloud-based storage. Data posted to the cloud is theoretically accessible to anyone who has access to the cloud. We are all familiar with the movie where the couple accidentally posts a racy video to the cloud. This is not merely a humorous plot device but a realistic aspect of the cloud. Whatever your personal opinions about the cloud are, cloud-based storage is not something that will be going away any time soon. Indeed, the cloud-based data market is estimated to have neared $200 billion in 2018.

The cloud is not just a place for you to store your data. Sure, the cloud is an effective data repository, but because many different types of data can be stored on the cloud, the possibility of this resource being used for analytical purposes now becomes real and important. This represents a change from the past where data might have been stored in a box, data had to be scanned, OCR (optical character recognition) had to be performed in order for the text in the documents to be recognized by software, and then a human being had to look at all this and interpret it.

Data migration to the cloud makes the cloud a resource that is capable of working with AI in important ways. As data is moving to the cloud much more rapidly than it has in the past, business leaders have to think about how they analyze their data. This represents the idea of data gravity where data services and analytics are drawn in the same direction as the data. With this rapid data migration, companies now have to think about how their employees access data and how they are able to use it in the field.

What this means for you as a business owner or business leader is that, yes, your data is in a place where it can be accessed more easily potentially by AI programs and staff, but that you also need to put thought into how your staff accesses previous data and stores new data. Perhaps you should invest in tablets that allow employees to access data on the cloud. Perhaps you can use tablets or other mobile devices to record new data, so that is instantly placed on the cloud rather than being transcribed on paper, scanned, et cetera.

Trend 5. Driving organizational change by making data more widely available

There is this idea of data democratization, which is perhaps more controversial than many acknowledge. Although it may be obvious to many that data is important and that companies need to think about what they are doing with their data if they want to keep up with their competitors who certainly are thinking about their data, what some overlook is the idea that questions of the commercial aspects of the data and who has access to the data are important.

We all interact with data. Our mobiles phones and other mobile devices have data plans that clearly state how much data we can exchange over a given period of time. Men and women using these devices exchange data in ways that most are not even conscious of. For example, as long as your mobile device has an internet connection, it is likely exchanging data. It may be interacting with a server to determine if the operating system or apps need to be updated. It may even be sending location or other information about you to private companies or to government agencies that are keeping track of this data.

What this means at the organization level, at least for business leaders, is that the question of making data available to employees in various ways needs to be talked about. The day and age of the IT guys being the only ones who were able to access certain types of data are long in the past. For one thing, many workers in today's tech companies (or any commercial operation for that matter) have enough of a computer science background that they are able to understand applications of the data and contribute to the conversation of how the data should be used.

What this means for you is that it may behoove you to make certain types of data more widely available in your company. All of this can be done with AI. By making data more widely available (democratizing it), you allow staff with ideas about how the data can be used to contribute to the business in ways that they have not before. Although we have spoken a lot in this book about how machine learning in AI allows the AI itself to learn, analyze, and predict, because the AI is involved in storing the data to some degree human beings who are able to access the data are also in the position to analyze and male recommendations that may be of use to the business.

Trend 6. Using data analytics for engagement

It is possible to write pages and pages on the subject of why businesses need to use AI for data analytics. The objective good for a business that comes with the adoption of AI for business intelligence is an assumption that many sources (including this book) make. But another question that companies need to ask is how data can be used for other means, like engaging their employees.

Adoption and engagement do not need to be at odds with each other, but there is the common belief in companies that if data is widely available somewhere like a cloud and that many employees have access to it this is a good thing. First of all, we do have to recognize that we just spent several paragraphs talking about the good that comes from making data available to employees more widely than it might have been previously. Yes, the adoption of cloud platforms and analytical data software is important. But the next step then becomes what this data means to the employees.

This is another aspect of the idea of democratization using AI. Employees may have access to the data, but who is making the decisions? Are AI programs using the data making decisions? Are business leaders making decisions? Are the employee foot soldiers who now have access to the data playing more of a role in decision-making now that they can see aspects of the company that they perhaps had not seen before?

Perhaps a way to think about it is this: if a new group of employees is able to access earnings reports that they had not been able to access before, does that mean that they are being engaged in this discussion in ways that they were not before? Perhaps the reports should be obtained differently. Perhaps there is information that should be gathered and is not being gathered, or, conversely, data that is being gathered that is no longer necessary. Data analytics is only useful to the extent that you can use it to affect company change, and this trend toward using data analytics for engagement of employees will only grow more important over time.

Trend 7. Team approach to data insights and applications

We are not quite at the point yet where artificial intelligence is at the point where it is not only storing, analyzing, and learning from the data, but it is making all of the company decisions. At the present time, the idea that AI should be used to analyze data and make recommendations is pretty standard, but it still is left to the business leaders to make the decisions and implement the change. In other words, maybe your company should cut down production of units on product one and instead make more of product two, but the AI agent is not doing this on its own. It is still the choice of the business leaders to do this or not to do this.

An alternative to simply allowing business leaders to be the ones involved in decision-making is to use data as a tool for communication, specifically in terms of insights gained from the data and how the data is to be applied. This storytelling represents a holistic approach to the data, representing what the data means to the company as a whole. Again, this also represents a type of democratization within the company because it means that data is not merely the preserve of the ones in charge, but that the employees have a stake in the data as well.

Recognizing employees as stakeholders in the company (and the data) is certainly a trend that is coming to characterize the convergence of business intelligence and AI. This type of democratization, in which insights and applications of the data are shared with employees in such a way as to facilitate communication between business leaders and employees, perhaps is a recognition that employees may have an understanding of the data that others in the company may not have. As employees may potentially be younger and more data-savvy than business leaders, involving them in decisions about data applications can be important.

Another aspect of this is many startups that are making the most use of AI involve men and women who are in a similar age and education demographics and may already be inclined to be a little more democratic about what to do with the data in terms of the business. Most of these businesses thinking about data insights and applications are not law firms comprised of the seasoned attorneys who have and the paralegals and new attorneys that have not. A company thinking about these sorts of trends may be made up of employees who are used to running ideas off of each other either in the college setting or just as people used to managing information. It may certainly behoove your business to use AI to incorporate this sort of practice into the way you do things.

Trend 8. Improved management of data improves the incorporation of data into business practices

Data is being used to motivate decisions in businesses, at a business leader level, and at an employee level. This is perhaps the power of AI: that it is becoming ubiquitous not only in business but in human life. We use AI to figure out how long it will take our significant other to drive to our house based on the distance between their house and ours. Do we have time to meet that friend from college for pizza or do we perhaps need to resort to reheating leftovers in the microwave instead?

Sure, this seems like an irrelevant decision, but it is a decision that is being driven by data. What happens when all of the decisions are driven by data obtained from AI? Recognize in this example that the AI is not merely spitting out data that it has stored somewhere. The AI actually has to make a sort of analysis (in the form of a calculation) to figure out a real distance between two points, meaning that the data is being handled or manipulated by AI to some degree.

The data that is accessed by AI technology, therefore, needs to be accurate and useful in order to be used to drive good decisions in the business. Thought about data management or data curation, therefore, becomes important because data represents the bridge that separates the business from its goals. Although it may seem obvious that AI needs to take the data being curated and analyze it in a particular way to be used, it is necessary for companies to invest in how they program AI to be able to perform these analyses. In other words, companies need to spend money to make sure that AI is doing the right things with the data.

Therefore, the trend becomes linking improved methods of data storage with business application tools. Although this subject can become very involved at the technical level, the AI technology basically requires data definitions which are then integrated with the tools that analyze the data. This not only serves the purpose of allowing the data to be analyzed in such a way that the AI can make the right predictions or recommendations, but it also permits the data to be understood by the human beings who still need to interact with the data. As this trend demonstrates, the day and age where human beings are extraneous to the data and AI interface are still far off yet.

Trend 9. Data collaboration leads to community good

The concept of data for good refers to the idea that data can have a good impact on the world, whether in the form of non-governmental organizations (NGOs) having access to data for humanitarian projects or private companies using the data to perform research that leads to community good. For example, private companies with access to large data caches can analyze data about public health, literacy, and other areas that can then be used to make decisions that improve quality of life in those areas.

Data for good is becoming increasingly important in the AI world. Research suggests that mentions of the term on social media have increased dramatically in the last year. There are many ways in which data can be used for projects that lead to community good. We have spent much of this chapter talking about data storage and curation, but something as simple as establishing a data platform where not-for-profits can access data represents a type of collaboration that can generate a positive end result.

This does not mean that the cloud does not have any use in data collaboration. Indeed, the cloud may represent data sharing par excellence, even for purposes that do not directly lead to profit. Much research has been done on how the cloud can form sort of a data commonwealth in which data is used to benefit large numbers of people in different ways. This represents a partnership between businesses, NGOs, technology creators, and educational institutions with the end goal of using data for good.

Although the focus of businesses has often been how they can protect their data from encroachment by individuals who they feel should not have access to the data, data collaboration takes the conversation in a different direction. This conversation implicitly recognizes that companies may have a social obligation when it comes to data, especially since they may be capable of extrapolating information from the data (for good) that other (including governments) are not able to.

Of course, the cynical approach is that the idea of a data commonwealth spearheaded by companies that store data represents sort of good publicity on the part of companies that house lots of private data about users (and even non-users). As the public becomes increasingly aware that companies store lots of data about them - whether it's pictures, personal information, or other private information - data collaboration efforts (like a cloud that is accessible to non-commercial entities) represents a trend that companies on the lookout for important industry changes need to be conscious of.

Trend 10. Understanding data with actionable analytics

Actionable analytics represents a few ideas important to a business. It represents the ability of a business to perform analysis of data and then to act on it. It also represents the idea of integrating data storage, analysis, and action into one place. For example, data that is accessed and analyzed on a computer or mobile device could potentially be acted on using the same device. This allows employees to take action immediately after accessing data and learning information. The alternative would be that insight is gained and the employee has to plan to take action.

There are several examples of how data analytics can be tied or embedded into a data utility. Software like SharePoint allows embedded analytics to occur: data that has been stored can be used to complete an important company action. Anyone familiar with SharePoint would therefore recognize that embedded data and actionable analytics are really not as complex as they sound. They really represent the recognition that data stored on intelligent platforms where the data can be manipulated in some way allow this "embedded" information to be acted on now instead of later.

It should not be difficult to understand why actionable analytics is becoming an important trend in business intelligence. Actionable intelligence not only allows companies to reduce the likelihood that important actions are not overlooked or forgotten, but they also reduce the time it takes to get from insight to action. Actionable analytics also democratizes data somewhat by allowing the individual with access to the data to act on it as long as they have the right permissions. As with other trends, this one requires that the data has been migrated to a platform where it can be acted on appropriately.

These trends are important for a reason. They represent an appreciation for what AI can do when it comes to businesses being able to apply their knowledge. At the heart of all of these trends is the importance of data. Data that has been written on a piece of paper stashed in a box somewhere is of no use to a business. It cannot be analyzed by AI technology, and it cannot result in an application that can improve the business. Business intelligence means using technology to keep your business competitive, and the first step towards doing that is being smart about your data.

Chapter 8 How AI is Changing the Job Market

All Jobs Will Be Replaced

Let's cut to the chase because every time that this topic comes up, it's really associated with the job that's being replaced. The problem with this topic is that people see the short-term result of what a specific technology will do. The truth of the matter is that all of the jobs in current existence will be replaced, given enough time. It is extremely easy to define and put into place machines for cooking hamburgers. The fact that we refrigerate hamburgers that are pre-made proves this point. Machines can already do most of the basic work that we need them to do.

It is not difficult to automate something, but what is difficult is choosing what needs to be automated. If you have ever talked to an accountant before, you will find that most businesses have different situations for their financial needs. It may be very easy to replace the hamburger maker or the cook in the kitchen with a robot, but it is much more difficult to replace the person who can assess the situation. The challenge with artificial intelligence is that it doesn't have something that allows it to understand context.

Whenever you go to pay your bills, you may not pay your bills on time on purpose. In an automated system, the bills will be paid on time every time. However, you may need to wait a week to pay a specific bill because of a certain reason. Tons of people delay paying bills because of reasons and so one problem that robots have is understanding context, the reason why something is being done. This means that even though all jobs will eventually be replaced, the jobs that will be replaced last are the jobs that require context. You cannot automate the process of building a full-scale website, you can automate the design process, the building blocks, and many of the different elements of a full-scale website but that website changes based on the company needs.

Even the Creative Jobs

This means that eventually even the creative jobs will be replaced once artificial intelligence machines can understand context. Here's the problem though; why does it matter? Why does it matter that jobs will be replaced? Jobs exist so as to continue our survival and basically to give us something to do until we die. It's not really a bad thing if all the mandatory jobs are replaced by robots because there is always going to be something else to do. Okay so you don't have to make hamburgers, but you can choose to create a shop of human-made food. That will become a specialty, shops that pride themselves on using only Human Services. Sure, you could automate a car fully, but a car is not going to speed down a runway at top speed to give you a drill thrill. Robots are designed to repeat repetitive tasks, things that you do for fun are things that only humans can do will exist. Only humans can make human made food or human made clothing, something that will be seen as the new fashion style. The job market is always going to exist and there will always be something to do, you just have to have the right perspective.

What do you need to know to implement A.I.?

Easier Than Ever

The first thing to know and understand is that you are standing on the shoulders of giants. A lot of people don't like to start out with this because they might think it's a little arrogant, but if you are just getting into artificial intelligence then you need to understand this. There has been a lot of work done in the past two decades regarding artificial intelligence, which means you are going to need to do a lot to get to where the frontier is at. That isn't to say that you can't do it within a reasonable time, it's just that you need to appreciate the complexity of this industry. Additionally, you need to understand that it has taken a lot of work to make things easy and while there are very easily implementable tools out on the market, understanding the core mechanics of how neural networks work is key to using these tools. The tools simply allow an individual to get the work they need done without having to deal with much hassle, understanding how those tools work is still something you're going to need.

Algebra to Calculus

The second thing that you're going to need to know is a variety of mathematical skills depending on what you want your artificial intelligence to do. If you want your artificial intelligence to simply forecast the next week's stock prices, you'll mostly need to know statistics as well as maybe a little calculus. If, on the other hand, you want to utilize artificial intelligence to generate 3D pieces of Art then you may need some geospatial mathematics along with a little bit of discrete mathematics. There is a wide range of mathematical skills that may be required depending on what you want to do with it, but the reason why I specifically state algebra to calculus is because you will at least need to know algebra. Neural networks are designed with the understanding of the slope-intercept form as the most basic form of a neural node. It only gets much more complicated after that. Most of your learning will actually be solely mathematical and very little of it will be programming, but that is the third thing that you need to know.

Programming

You will need to understand programming to the degree of the tool that you plan to use. If you are going to a website that allows you to use a neural network that was already built beforehand, you're likely not going to need much programming. If you plan to utilize a localized version of a neural network, you are probably going to need to know how to program and access the graphics processor unit Library that's compatible on your computer. A lot of people misunderstand this requirement because in the beginning they are thinking about DirectX 11 or 12 or maybe a Vulcan architecture, but these are graphical libraries. If you plan to create a localized neural network, you will need to know a significant bit about the hardware that you plan to use. This is because you can use the central processing unit or the graphical processing unit to do the job, but how you go about using it is definitely different.

Which jobs will be replaced the soonest?

Repetitive Tasks Are the First to Go

As I have mentioned several times at this point, the first jobs that are going to go are the ones that can be repeated. Flipping hamburgers, filing, writing checks, lifting things, stocking things, ensuring things are on shelves, and pretty much anything that requires a routine. That's almost all of the low-end jobs; the ones that teenagers and the elderly tend to find themselves at. These jobs will be the first to go because you don't need to pay wages to a robot and all you need to do is maintain the robot to extract the benefits. You will still need somebody in a managerial position to handle customers, but generally, all the basic jobs can be robot.

Now, it is important to understand that there will still be one person left to just be there. This is sort of like the individual that is there at the self-checkout. The individual is not really supposed to make sure that you are checked out and get all your groceries, they are there should anything go wrong. These jobs will become the new jobs that teenagers and elderly fit instead of the ones that require the person to check out. This means that Mom and Pop shops will probably still hire the person willing to look after the register during the business hours, but a company like Walmart or Target is likely going to hire one person to manage stocking robots.

There will also be an increase in need for Maintenance Technicians and Maintenance Engineers, to ensure that the robots are properly maintained.

Jobs carried out via Rules Go Second

We've already begun seeing jobs that require rules begin to have their own version of replacements installed. For instance, as I mentioned before there is now a contract lawyer artificial intelligence that would essentially replace lawyers that focused specifically on contract work. These positions primarily follow rules and patterns, which means that even though it is significantly more difficult in routine than compared to stocking something on the shelf, it can still be automated given enough work.

Consultancy Goes Third

The last type of job that will go is consultancy and the reason why I say this is because consultancy is a routine but contextual job. Sure, you could say that in consultancy all you are doing is judging what can be added or subtracted from a workload so that the company makes more money. This is something that a machine can currently do, but the problem comes in the form of contextual understanding. You see, any machine can go and create optimization methods for a business, but the business has to create that machine to fit that business. This means that the business itself is providing the contextual understanding the business needs in order to make an effective evaluation of what is needed to optimize the business. When a person comes in to consult for a business, they need to understand the business before they begin suggesting anything. This necessity for a contextual understanding is something that can't be quantified by a machine just yet and so this is why that will be the last type of job to go. However, ultimately, it will eventually go.

Which jobs are least likely to be replaced?

Inventors

The primary job that will not be replaced, I repeat it will not be replaced is an inventor. An inventor is an individual who thinks outside of the box. They look at the market and they look at what available tools exist before they begin generating ideas for what can exist if you combine those tools. The reason why an inventor will not be replaced is because almost all companies require an inventor in order to begin a company in the first place. They are the thing that drives the industry. They absorb more data than any current processor or processor within the next decade would be able to sustain and abstract into an invention. In other words, inventors don't have any rules beyond the rules of the universe. This means that you can't automate the job because there is nothing to automate.

Frontier Science

The next type of job that is not likely going to see any form of automation is Frontier science and this is primarily due to the fact that scientists want to keep machines away from science. That isn't to say that there won't be a lot of science that these machines are capable of and it isn't to say that these machines won't be helping to march forward in the frontier science, but machines are not likely to be the entity to march forward in the frontier science. There's too much mistrust of machines, there is too much paranoia around the singularity, and if we hand over science to the machines then there will be nothing left for Humanity to do.

Will Universal Basic Income fix the problem?

Giving Everyone a Base Income

The idea of universal basic income is to give everyone a base income so that no one starves to death. This idea is not new and in fact, a lot of communist countries, as well as some socialist countries, believe in basic income for everyone in society. Due to the rapid replacement of jobs that might occur as a result of technology, many of the top leaders in technology have begun suggesting a universal basic income to offset the job loss. This would be provided on a global scale so that everyone could better their lives and it's a really good ideal but not a good idea.

Here is the concept in a nutshell because I have to describe more than what Universal basic income is as to why the leaders of Technology would believe in such an idea... I mean bad idea. If everyone loses their job, no one has to suffer because people can still buy things if they have money. In order to ensure that they have this money, the richest people in the world donate so that everyone has a base income. This base income level would ensure that people could buy the bare necessities that they needed in order to live. This would not fix the problem of job loss, but it would significantly decrease the harmful impact that the job lost would have on the average individual because that individual would be able to buy food and similar items that would stimulate the economy.

Companies Pass Cost to Customer

The problem is that the world doesn't work like that. You cannot have a society that was previously based off of meritocracy immediately converge into a community that shares everything, it just doesn't work. I'm not saying that the idea of a universal basic income is impossible, what I am saying is that when you spend centuries building a society towards always making more and not sharing, it becomes incredibly difficult to become a community that shares everything. Universal basic income would cause companies to pass the cost of that base income to the customer by making products more expensive. The problem is that you now are automating most of the jobs that currently exist, firing employees that would have made more than the universal basic income, and now you have an influx of people who receive your money to buy your products.

Devalue the Currency

When you inflate the value of a currency, it will almost immediately depreciate in value. Let's say that we decided to put in the universal basic income and companies passed the cost on to the customer. You now have everyone at the same pay level if they don't have a job, however, money is limited. You may give them all a base pay grade, but the money is limited so unless you're going to print more money than you would have to take the money of the rich. If you take the money of the rich, the rich don't have any incentive to build new companies to become even richer if that just means you're going to take more of their money. On the opposite side, if you decided to print a lot of money you would devalue the currency. Printing money inflates how much money you have in society and this money is actually a representation of Exchange. Imagine that you had 10 tickets that you could trade in for a $300 guitar. Each of those tickets is worth $30. Now, printing money is the same as printing more tickets so let's say that you print more tickets and now you have 20 tickets for the same $300 guitar. Now, each ticket is worth about $15. Therefore, based on the example, you can pretty much see why printing more money makes money more worthless.

Everything is Now the Same but Worse

So now that you have seen the concept and you see what results from it in a very, extremely simplistic example, you can see why this is a bad idea. Sure, in the first month, maybe, the base income becomes useful but every month after that you have companies passing the cost on to the customer and then you have the worst, which is that the money that pays the cost lowers in value. This causes everything to become more expensive and the base income value is now pointless because everything you could have bought with the base income to survive is now more expensive. Therefore, everything is mostly the same but worse because now what you're getting paid is worth less than it was originally. This is why universal basic income simply doesn't work and why it has failed every society that has tried to use it.

Chapter 9 The Future of AI in Business

While the organizations make attempts to manage wide-ranging information and a growing range of gadgets, still quality decisions can be made on the basis AI and the IoT due to a couple of new techniques.

Jane, a marketing specialist is working with her team members on a presentation for a new business. The client is a gigantic business conglomerate, and the presentation team is sustaining growing pressure to get the account.

Besides, Jane data collection process is complex. She obtains data from her co-workers who are located remotely and send information through emails, phone calls, and via WhatsApp and instant messaging. She is simultaneously searching online data for completion of her assignment.

In 2020, approximately 7.6 billion people will expectedly make up the world population. In the same year, the IoT connected devices are also expected to rise from 20 to30 billion. In this scenario, how can Jane and hundreds of thousands of other people handle this much information, how they can decide what is vital besides making a right decision in these circumstances?

If these gadgets and human resources are figured out, we can observe an exponential rise of data and this abundant information is already producing 'infoxication.'

Artificial intelligence apparently is one of the smart solutions to all of these challenges, where certain tools are developed that have potential to cope with information besides searching for reliable data sources. Moreover, informed decision making and improved cognition are other benefits.

Workplace hub generally focuses on the office, and particularly on the imminent workplaces. It makes use of a single centralized platform and combines all of an organization's technology. Also, this improves the productivity by curtailing the IT related expenditure.

It delivers real-time insights through which business processes are transformed. With the acceptance of IoT and AI systems, workplace hub will be transformed in upcoming time to turn out to be a cognitive hub.

The intelligent edge computing and AI will be merged by this new technology. Besides increasing association between individuals and teams, human intelligence will ultimately be augmented to expand the network of human interfaces.

Within the digital sector, Cognitive Hub will serve a dynamic platform for information flows and it will offer augmented intelligence for masses at large.

Moreover, it will integrate future gadgets, such as: flexible screens, augmented reality glasses and smart-walls. For incorporating wisdom, Cognitive Hub will utilize AI to gather and process data with an aim to bring comfort for, individuals, teams and companies.

According to some people, cloud computing will vanish, but the fact is it will persist. Rather, it will diverge and become a cortex-like structure made of complex three-dimensional tree. Today, cloud computing is a bond among cognitive computing, intelligent automation and other AI driven fields.

Huge work is yet to deliver in the cognitive hub; however, our working style has already been transformed by workplace hub and it enables us to control the growing intensification in information and gadgets.

Future of AI in 2020

Speaking of 'Millenials' and the generations to come, the modern-day discoveries do distinguish us from our ancestors. So far, human minds have invented created simulations of almost everything. Brain was and it is the only common thing among us, our ancestors and the impending generation, which transforms our communication, thinking styles and working patterns. Researchers have predicted Artificial Intelligence since long. However, it was initially bonded with robots only. Today, AI has been integrated into almost everything in our use. AI is considered to be software application, which pretends to behave like humans.

It is a blessing in this modern day and age, since it has brought ease and comfort in the lives of humans, it facilitates us in early completion of tasks. In this way, minimum energies are consumed, time is saved and the work gets accomplished efficiently.

Programming

This has taken us to new world of wonders, where things are taking place beyond our imaginations. AI provides us the connectivity and acts as continuity among discrete actions. We can say that you can interact with numerous things at one point of time, such as rapid conversion from one language to another. With the early introduction of computers, we have been following certain procedures for dealing with our actions, which can be customized from settings menu. These rules are not required while transferring the same technology into AI. Rather, algorithm is trained to associate with the course of actions.

Predictions 2019

We come across a number of variables in Artificial intelligence and all the variables are enabled to be processed in a programmatic style, which is quite easy and it offers an evident understanding and confidence of transparent nature. It is debatable; however, prediction of the future happenings can be accurate, if done within the scientific field of data. Since the beginning, computers were believed to handle the all the numerical and statistical jobs. The foundation of machine learning is computation of the statistical importance and it plays a key role in predicting weather patterns, diagnosing diseases and playing chess. As we are always proceeding further towards high processing power and data volume, for which the computer-based tasks driven by algorithms are appropriate.

Decisions

Depending on data extracted from management information systems, decisions today are made by the companies, since data is directly materialized from company operations, as a result of which it is challenging to either make or break the rules. Decision making gets refined with the implementation of AI into the decision supporting tools. While defining customer data into predictive models, decision management technologies are also fostered by the proficiencies in AI. On the basis of the major demographics, other departments such as consumer and marketing are transforming their efforts because of this new trend.

In other words, it is a developed technology supported by digital banking, and, various enterprise applications are currently using this technology.

Interactions

With the minimal effort, new forms of the interface are generated by the AI. The invention of mouse and keyboards has made us use these gadgets in our routine lives and we are still the users of keyboard and mouse. As far as digital communications are concerned, we have learned to design and develop the algorithms for benefits realization. We can observe a natural and smooth interaction, as the codes can now be transformed into human sentences and suspend the input from cameras and sensors.

What You Should Expect with Future of AI Technology?

Our actions, thoughts and living styles are being reshaped due to several technological innovations; however, the remarkable changes are delivered by the AI. While AI has recently penetrated the market, the AI has become flexible due to the modern revolutions. Evaluating its future, an individual can observe an environment where each aspect of our lives is controlled by the AI.

Most Promising AI Innovations

Generally, our whole life will be reshaped through the AI acceptance. While, we are seeking AI driven tools at home, the corporations, businesses, and administrations are still using it.

Introduction of self-driving cars on the road is a big example. While this industry is expected to grow, regulations and policies to control AI-driven vehicles are being made by the U.S transport department.

AI in the field of transportation aims to develop self-driving cars. At present, AI has achieved the hallmark of designing the human-driven automatic cars and is expected to soon achieve self-driving cars with no human intervention.

To develop self-driving planes and buses, AI is still the major focus of many firms and transport sector.

AI and Robotics will Integrate

AI has already been integrated with cybernetics, which is an ongoing progress. With the integration of AI technology into robotics, the human beings will be able to improve their bodies with strength and endurance. While we may improve our bodies with introduction of cybernetics, the disabled people could better realize its benefits. Life of the persons with amputated limbs or permanent paralysis can be improved.

AI will Create Complete Functional Robots

Nexus to above, we can build artificial life-forms as a result of AI technology. The knowledge of human-like robots capable of performing complex interactions has been extensively discovered by the science fiction. Robots can have diverse significance as the field of robotics is being transformed with presence of AI. For instance, robots can perform a risky task and take action, which otherwise may be unsafe for humans.

Impact on Humans

Gartner released some figures that 1.8 million jobs will be eradicated by the AI with the replacement of 2.3 million jobs by 2012. By observing this drive starting from earlier 3 industrial revolutions to this digital one, it is observed that there has been a considerable transformation in our lives and working styles and same would continue in upcoming times. Take the example of a world, where people will work only two days a week. Such a time is soon expected.

However, AI is a big-big deal with these synthetic elements. Now, we live in realism, because, in light of better learning, we are familiar with the rapid completion of task with maximum precision.

With automated reasoning as a positive glow in employment, 2020 will significantly witness the business advancement in AI.

The mark of almost two million net-new services is expected to be hit by AI based occupations till 2025.

A momentary employment misfortune has been associated with the different advancements; however, soon it is recovered by the benefits offered by these advancements. The business will change at that point, and this course will probably be taken by AI. The effectiveness of multiple occupations will be improved by the AI, doing away with several center and low-level positions.

Future of AI in Workplace

AI and IOT are not only making our homes smart. Rather they are penetrating into a number of businesses besides interrupting the places of work. The efficiency, productivity, and accuracy within a company can be changed due to AI.

Nonetheless, many people are afraid that due to AI progression, robots will replace the human workers and the same is perceived as a threat instead of a tool to transform our-selves.

With the continuing dialogues of AI back in 2018, it should be understood by the businesses that black-box potential and self-learning are not the solution in this modern era. With realization of AI based benefits to see value addition and to improve human intelligence, the unlimited power of AI is being experienced by many organizations.

Several decision-makers have begun using the capabilities of AI, because the advantages of intelligent systems are supported by significant evidences. According to a research work by EY, organizations integrating AI at the enterprise level see two main benefits: efficiency enhancement and informed decision making.

The competitive advantage is gained by the company who is pioneer in implementing AI. Since it can curtail the recurring expenditures and may reduce other head counts. This is a positive element in terms of business perspective, but people in different work places are likely to be taken over by machines, which is not an encouraging thing. Some conflict between machines and humans will obviously be created with the introduction of AI.

In the presence of innovative systems, our economy will greatly be affected by the AI with the creation of skillful jobs.

It is likely that AI will be emerged to replace certain jobs entailing iterative tasks and resultantly the current human ability will be concealed. The place of humans will be decided by the AI tools.

The tasks, such as: detecting corruption, loan approval and financial crime will be executed by the automated decisions.

Owing to the development in automation, an enhancement in production levels will be witnessed by the organizations.

How to Maximize AI?

Since the AI progression will affect a number of jobs, it is also better to observe some of the problems that AI may take along.

- By identifying an effective implementation, a solution to the bias problem around AI should be discovered by the business.

- The government should ensure that the profits of AI should be equally shared among the affected people and those unaffected by the developments.

The issues must be addressed at an informative level to successfully obtain benefits of AI. The students can be empowered in AI related tasks as a result of educational systems.

Consequently, much importance is required to be given to STEM subjects. In addition, we should inspire the subjects enhancing innovation and emotional abilities. Although, compared to humans, artificial intelligence will be productive, humans are always found efficient in performing better than machines and across jobs where relationship building and resourcefulness are needed.

The domain outside and inside the workplace will be transformed by the artificial intelligence. Rather than emphasizing on the fear of automation, the technologies should be happily accepted by the businesses to ensure that the successful AI systems are to be implemented for enhancing and supplementing the human intelligence.

Ensuring that Machines Don't Take Over

When the likelihood of certain technology to take over the world was signaled by Stephen Hawking, then it seemed right to ponder over it.

In 2014, Hawking stated that the human race could be ended as a result of AI. World has witnessed countless benefits, because human intelligence is one of the elements yielded in every discovery. Predicting the accomplishments and milestones we shall achieve upon implementation of these AI based tools is a hard thing, but we cannot undermine the eradication of poverty and ailment.

Since long, world has seen humanity's potential death at the hands of machines. A PWC's March 2017 economic report depicts and foresees that machines will take over nearly 30 percent of UK jobs by 2030. Those at risk could possibly be the people in the storage, transportation, manufacturing and retail sectors.

A few people maintain a different opinion contrary to this chilling report by PWC. For instance, Accenture estimates that an additional $814billion will be realized by the UK economy as a result of AI technologies.

Many miserable and terrible stories exist about AI, and the job displacement effect has heavily been emphasized by various studies. Though, this might be believed as a simplistic view according to many people.

The GDP is no more being enhanced by the conventional boosters of financial growth, but the rays of hope are brought by the AI.

In this regard, experts are of view that a new shape of virtual labor is AI, which can successfully overcome the traditional market and can change the precursors of growth.

The intelligent automation and augmentation will be fostered by the AI. Both are different concepts. The former entails the application of data to deliver services besides smart execution of tasks. While, the latter one accepts the things and enables us to perform them in an efficient manner.

The increase in cloud availability and the rising cost of computer power has stimulated AI in the business industry. The companies and governments worldwide are implementing cloud-based platform to analyze the network of data in near-real time.

Each bit of data can be stored and amalgamated with these algorithms to bring about a novel and miraculous opportunity.

You cannot convince your senior executives to advance, if a mathematics professor is needed to assist you with explanation of ML and AI algorithms.

By creating applications depending upon the fundamental technology, this has been accomplished by Ayasdi, but main goal was to concentrate on business challenges like identifying the best practices in healthcare from the hospital data so that the best quality care could be delivered on affordable amount.

AI providers are already extending their help to the organizations in becoming efficient and smarter. The AI technologies can yield in huge financial potential, but how the infrastructure and human resource could be developed and trained to realize the economic gain.

In future, traditional jobs will be eclipsed by the technology driven jobs, where you will probably be guiding the robots or getting work done from machine. This is the time when we have to educate the people to become ready for the upcoming challenges.

Things to Note about Future of AI

1. AI is considerably outreaching beyond our imaginations

2. The artificial intelligence is in daily use by many people

Some of the general examples of AI are Cortana and Siri. AI is expanding everywhere. The video games, cars, lawnmowers and vacuum cleaners are witnessing the use of AI. In addition, some other example may include international financial markets, E-commerce software, and medical research domains.

3. Robots will Take over Part of Your Job

You might be exhibiting good performance in your job. However, many of the office-based workflows have been automated or will be automated in due course. As per Professor Moshe Vardi of the Rice University, most jobs will be carried out by robots after 3 decades. That might not sound good, but many researchers are of the view that this will be a new beginning when work will be done with pleasure and not out of need.

4. Many Intelligent People believe Building AI to Human Level is Risky Thing to Do

A lot of disturbing things can happen, when machines behave like humans. A small likelihood exists that expansion of AI will stop very soon.

5. If AI Gets Smarter Than Us, Then We Have Little Chance of Learning It

Super intelligent devices perform working ahead of our thoughts. It may take years and years to gain an insight with these simplest things it is familiar with, but there will be no valuable result.

6. Super Intelligent AI could Work because of Three Techniques

7. Reason Why We Have Never Met Aliens Could Be None Other Than AI

Intelligent Future

That time is arriving soon, when the conventional jobs will be obscured by intelligent machines coupled with the human-like robots and the high power of modern computing technology.

Nonetheless, in some scenarios, AI programs deliver better output than the humans, like pattern recognition tasks and playing video games. These are simply the iterative tasks which machines could do better and humans fail to compete with machine intelligence in such scenarios.

It took decades and decades by human brains to evolve from simple things to advanced cutting-edge technologies besides performing productive functions. Intelligence of humans and those of machines cannot go in parallel.

We can learn the processing of information from the simple animal brains. For instance, despite lacking a forebrain, a certain level of intelligence is also exhibited by the trivial animals like octopus and bees.

Compared to AI, the performance of these animals is better, since they can carry out diverse tasks by taking minimal time. Basically, millions of samples are needed by deep learning networks prior to learning.

To conclude, artificial intelligence is gaining widespread fame across almost all the occupations. For example, growth of AI has reportedly higher since 2018. Nowadays, people have started to acknowledge AI is being acknowledged by a large number of people owing to the benefits it provides in the personal and professional life of humans. The common benefit of AI is that it generates the desirable outputs to humans while curtailing cost, reducing time and giving amazing experiences.

Conclusion

The idea of imitating human mind with the help of symbolic structures and operations is the basis of Artificial Intelligence. Besides the fact that Artificial Intelligence can lead various businesses to a new level, there is still an argument if Artificial Intelligence can replace human intelligence and behave like it. But to take advantage from the benefits of AI, one should not wait for the resolution of these controversies.

There was a time, when information technology was used to automate the processes and to compute business philosophies. But, now the more important thing is the vision and how this vision can help in creating a value and to achieve the desired goals in a presence of competing environment. All this can be achieved by acquiring Artificial Intelligence. With the help of AI, possibilities of getting to the top position in today's business world will be endless. Soon every industry will start to get help from AI and ML to make their business models effective and efficient. One can easily see that AI is ready to change the methods of doing businesses.

You have to have a vision if you want to acquire Artificial Intelligence for your business. But you need to get rid of same old traditional ideas and equip yourself with upgraded approach for your organization and for your AI application. This book serves the same purpose. It will give you an introduction of the most up-to-date techniques and analytics that will help you to strategize your company's processes effectively. Also, you will be guided about the different ways that are most suitable for your company's goals. It is worth mentioning that business sectors like manufacturing, sports, banking, and retails have already started to get help from machine learning and AI.

Machines are now more technologically advanced and are able to complete complex task with great precision and attention to detail. However, it is noteworthy that a machine's true potential depends completely on the amount of data fed into its system. So far, neural networks have contributed tremendously in the field of AI. The customization of input data and its role in improving the quality and performance of the available products makes one hopeful about the future of AI. The ever-growing field of machine learning indicates that we'll be using a highly-developed AI earlier than we imagined. Until that happens, we hope this book would serve as a source of information for its readers.

CPSIA information can be obtained
at www.ICGtesting.com
Printed in the USA
LVHW031345100121
675965LV00003B/222